THE UNCOMFORTABLE CEO

MAKING INFORMATION TECHNOLOGY
OVERCOME BUSINESS UNCERTAINTY

Tom

Best reading and success! Yours,

José Ignacio

26/6/13

THE UNCOMFORTABLE CEO

MAKING INFORMATION TECHNOLOGY OVERCOME BUSINESS UNCERTAINTY

Windy City Publishers
2118 Plum Grove Rd., #349
Rolling Meadows, IL 60008
www.windycitypublishers.com

Published in the United States of America

10 9 8 7 6 5 4 3 2 1

First Edition: 2013

Library of Congress Control Number:
2013908690

ISBN:
978-1-935766-82-7

Windy City Publishers

CHICAGO

WINDY CITY

PUBLISHERS

¿Eres tú?
Si supieras quien escribe,
sabrías que es a ti a
quien escribo.

This book is dedicated to my sister Melita,
who fought the "Emperor of all Maladies,"
and her history of eureka moments and times of despair.
I hope she has found peace and eternal love at the end of her journey.
January 6, 2013

THE UNCOMFORTABLE CEO

MAKING INFORMATION TECHNOLOGY
OVERCOME BUSINESS UNCERTAINTY

José Ignacio Sordo Galarza

Foreword

by Jorge P. Montoya

The first time I met José Ignacio was way back in the late 1980s during one of my business trips to Mexico City. At that time, I was the regional president of the Procter & Gamble Company. This young Sales Technology supervisor had masterminded a breakthrough proposal and wanted to show it to his executive leadership team. If approved, he was planning to go national with the first-ever analytical engine to track historical sales data using IBM personal desktops. (For perspective, at that time, only certain executives and very few salespeople were permitted to request "data dumps" from our IT department and then had to wait for two or three days for the printed report to arrive at their office via inter-office correspondence.) His digital proposal got the entire executive leadership team interested. He vividly reminded me of Tom Robbins' quote from *Still Life with Woodpecker*: "Humanity has advanced, when it has advanced, not because it has been sober, responsible, and cautious, but because it has been playful and rebellious." Almost three decades later, José Ignacio is still rebellious and innovative…

José Ignacio recently asked me to comment on his business book. This is what I told my spouse after the unexpected phone call: "Holy cow! You're not going to believe this—he wants me to foreword a book about information technology!" (Before I go any further, a quick disclaimer: I am certainly NOT an information technology expert.)

The truth of the matter is that he convinced me that this book is not about technical jargon or the latest IT buzz words nor is it a treatise on the latest information systems. Rather, he believes his ideas will resonate well within the business community. In short, his book is aimed at helping business leaders find the business relevance in IT by focusing on two goals:

- Explaining complex IT challenges in simple business terms.

- Creating and protecting the shareholder value of businesses.

I was intrigued and read the draft document. This is what I found:

- I very much enjoyed the tag line, "Making information technology overcome business uncertainty." It is meaningful and makes for rather interesting conversation about the real reason why all businesses (i.e., consumer goods, minerals, media, apparel, retailing, etc.) should approach the modern discipline of information technology.

- José Ignacio does not have "tunnel vision" about information technology. Each and every one of the nine chapters describes tough choices to make and hard work to do going forward. He proposes simple and concise leadership action to-do lists for the executives.

- Change is inevitable. The adaptive will survive, and the proactive will prevail. Innovation in information technology is the lifeblood of the twenty-first century. The business wins when discontinuities are created. Deep business understanding is a stimulus to innovation and a requisite for outstanding marketplace execution.

- There is an evident common theme throughout the entire book: "Value is the common ground for IT propositions that proactively deliver business relevance."

- Businesses must continue to make clear, sometimes difficult, information technology choices in their quest for consistently excellent performance.

Reading José Ignacio's book also gave me a huge sense of accomplishment—to have had the opportunity to lead so many young people to develop, grow, mature, and advance in business practice. That is something that no one can take away.

Perhaps your next move after reading this book will be to envision how you would like the future of the business and information technology to look in your own enterprise—let's say in a three- to five-year horizon—and then engage yourself and others into this vision. Defining a vision is particularly critical in times of uncertainty, to help people imagine what the future might bring and to keep them focused on tomorrow's possibilities rather than on today's obstacles. Once you have defined your plan, you can concentrate on validating your strategic choices and creating sufficiency plans to make it a reality.

I wish you great success in these endeavors.

Finally, this book is both thought provocative and helpful. If it challenges your thinking in a new way, then it has served its purpose!

~Jorge P. Montoya

JORGE P. MONTOYA is a member of the board of directors of Gap, Inc. and the Kroger Company in the USA and of Farmatodo in Venezuela. Previously, Jorge worked for the Procter & Gamble Company for thirty-three years. He retired in 2004 as President of Latin America and President of Global Snacks and Beverages. Jorge is a member of the advisory board of the Haas School of Business, University of California, Berkeley; the executive committee of the Youth Orchestra of the Americas (Washington DC); and the USA National Society of Hispanic MBAs. Jorge was selected as one of the "50 Most Important Hispanics in Business and Technology" in the United States in May 2003 by *Hispanic Engineer and Information Technology* magazine. He received the "Merit to Work Order" (First Class 1996), the "Francisco de Miranda Order" (First Class 1997); and the "Diego de Losada Order" (First Class 1999), all bestowed by the government of Venezuela. Jorge obtained his BS degree in mechanical engineering in 1969 and his MBA in 1971, both from the University of California, Berkeley. In 1994 he was selected to deliver the commencement speech to the graduating MBA and undergraduate classes of the UC Berkeley Haas Business School.

Acknowledgements

This book is the result of my thirty years of business experience. I am most enormously grateful to all the colleagues who have worked with me, at various times and in different industries. Throughout those years, I experienced the following:

- Two international relocations to live and work for extended periods and enriched with a hands-on exposure to diverse cultures in three continents;

- Resilience with endless failures and many sleepless working nights;

- Thrown into different situations, especially those in which I felt uncomfortable, and of course;

- Proud satisfaction with my team achievements.

I gratefully acknowledge the time and energy contributed by Bonnie Baker, who has shared her expertise in editing my original papers.

I am blessed to have friends who were kind enough to share their inspiration and support with their multiple revisions: José Angel Arias, Sanjog Aul, Militza Basualdo, Jorge L. Brake, Scott Bockheim, John Burrell, Victor Cedillo, Andy Chen, Polo Coronado, Sergio Coronado, Gerardo Diaz, Roland Dietz, Franz Dill, Luis Dominguez, José Alberto Esteve, Tarek Farahat, Ramón Galarza, José Luis Garza, Cyro Gazola, Jorge González Rico, José Guerra, Praveen Gupta, Raúl Heredia, Durward Hofler, Julio Ibarra, Juan Carlos Jaramillo, Ed Jardine, Bob Johansen, Rick Julien, Sandee Kastrul, Chris Kenny, Raúl Lamus, Haden Land, Rodrigo Leudo, Jorge López, Alfonso Luna, Jorge P. Montoya, Stefan Neff, Skip Newman, Mona Pearl, Hector Pliego, Moises Polishuk, Ana Rodríguez, Rodrigo Roque, Juan Luis Sánchez, Robert Scott, Steve Ungs, Tom Verdery, James Waite, Rob West, and Jorge Zavala, all of whom have been extremely generous with their time.

To my children, Santiago Iñaki, Amalia, and Juan Pablo for their patience while I wrote this book.

Finally, to my wife, Amalia, for her unconditional love and support in keeping me focused and working decisively to write this CIO Eureka! book.

contents

INTRODUCTION

Rerum primordia
~Lucretius (99BC–55BC)

Up to the 1990s, it was very easy to identify information technology companies. They were providers of technology gadgets, tools and software. You could easily find them with names such as IBM, HP, Microsoft, Dell and the late Burroughs and NCR. Starting in the 1990s, the creative Silicon Valley minds led a revolution with user-centric Internet services such as Google, eBay, Amazon, Yahoo, Facebook and other now-familiar names. But today, the truth of the matter is that every company is now an information technology company to some degree.

Regardless of the nature of your business, the geography in which you compete or in which you own market share, your company relies on information technology to operate, ranging from basic cost optimization, to digesting huge amounts of market data, running operations, transacting funds, designing products, streamlining processes, recruiting talent, commercializing business data and, wherever possible, transforming entire marketplaces. Information technology has become truly ubiquitous.

I would like to quote a key learning obtained from three memorable IT meetings during my consulting experience. The first one was actually a question. A key vendor turned to me and asked, "What's your comfort level with this idea?" The second was a statement by an associate in my own firm: "I know this is a powerful idea, but I feel a little uncomfortable with it." The third one was from a project manager planning to implement a new work process. She simply said, "I'm just not comfortable."

Those three separate observations, uttered in three separate meetings, had four things in common:

- They were all centered on the notion of comfort, and how important it is to be comfortable with an idea before you go ahead with it.

- Each one of those remarks turned out to be dead-end roads for an idea that just might have been a great one.

- In our business lives, we are going to have to choose between comfort and progress.

- I cannot think of a single progressive idea—in history, culture, business, or information technology—that was comfortable to contemplate when it was first proposed.

Disruptive ideas, almost by definition, have cutting edges. Cutting edges are rarely safe—and they are never comfortable. Disruptive ideas question the sanctity of old ideas—and questioning sanctity is not comfortable. Disruptive ideas are usually risky—and risk is almost always uncomfortable.

And yet, if the only decisions we ever made were the decisions with which we were comfortable, history would have unfolded differently. Columbus would never have discovered America because it can hardly have been comfortable to contemplate sailing off the edge of a flat world. Steve Jobs would never have revitalized Apple from near bankruptcy to profitability during his second CEO term because it cannot have been comfortable to create an entirely new market (e.g., "1,000 songs in your pocket" as he referred to the first iPod in 2001).

John E. Pepper (1.1) once wrote: "Embarking on something that you are not sure you can do—but being sure it is right and that you have to try—we have found that many of the most important things in life are like that."

Some business leaders are not comfortable with how information technology is changing their business model. But, it is not the job of a business leader to be comfortable! There's a dictum that says "Comfort breeds complacency, and complacency breeds failure." Complacent teams and organizations are on a slippery slope to self-destruction. Have you and your team become too comfortable?

This book explains how to find the objectivity and the perspective in business and information technology to make something positive happen. I will explore progressive ideas related to:

- Finding the business value of information technology;

- Improving shareholders return on information technology investments;

- Enhancing your time with your CIO and key IT associates;

- Practicing change management and adoption techniques;

- Leveraging information technology as an accelerator for collaboration and relationships—both key elements to fostering a culture of IT innovation in the marketplace.

The next time your IT leadership team presents you with a strategic plan, listen to the proposal and ask about three important things: 1) the business success criteria, 2) the change-management plan and, more importantly, 3) how to use this plan to establish IT as a true business leader for the entire company. Be careful not to pigeonhole the team and have it work on only technical issues. Make sure the team members understand the full scope of the business, and that they are working with you to transform the company. Tell them also that you are looking for counsel, but not for comfort. Nothing important ever happens when you are comfortable.

At the end of each chapter, I will share tips or recommended CEO leadership actions so that you can put your learning into practice.

I hope my experience will prove helpful in evolving your IT organization into perhaps the highest-leveraged function! And maybe—just maybe—the business lessons from this book will be valued.

Please do not hesitate to contact me at sordo@CIOEureka.com or www.CIOEureka.com should you require further assistance.

Best regards,

José Ignacio Sordo Galarza
July 2013

chapter one

Who Are the Uncomfortable CEOs?

The chief executive officer (CEO) is the highest-ranking executive in the corporation. CEOs are responsible for leading the development and execution of their company's long-term strategy with a view to creating shareholder value. They have a passion for winning and earning the trust and respect of their consumers, customers, employees and communities.

However, what differentiates a below average performance from an average or exceptional one? The strongest CEOs do approach work in a very consistent fashion: They get comfortable with being uncomfortable.

They are interested in *what* is right, rather than *who* is right; they have a general dissatisfaction with the status quo, and are always looking for ways to explore new boundaries. They all share the following virtues:

STRONG CURIOSITY

They travel and meet clients, consumers, thought-leaders and people in general across the marketplace in which their company competes. Leaders with a high level of innate curiosity discover invigorating opportunities; those without it find those same opportunities exhausting. These people have a critical and objective view of the imperfection and improbability of things. They have well-pondered and often strong points of view. At the same time, they are exceptionally attentive listeners and value diversity of thought.

THE ABILITY TO FACE REALITY

This quality helps them overcome the sense of isolation, tap into past networks and create new ones inside (and more importantly, outside) of their organizations to connect with ideas, advice, critical questioning, and sometimes precisely the support they need to move forward. They have the courage to act. In a nutshell, these leaders are able to make difficult decisions that are neither pleasant nor popular.

DRIVE FOR RESULTS

Learning and understanding new challenges and tensions that arise in any business is a necessary, albeit insufficient, step. These leaders develop far-reaching objectives and standards for their organization that go beyond those that might be adopted by the average person. They attach great importance to making a personal difference in all they do. They have pride of ownership in leading the company. They tend to expand the scope of their position. They are constantly on the outlook for new areas and new ways in which to contribute new ideas that can build volume and profit, as well as the organization's capacity (people). They combine tremendous personal initiative with respect for others.

NEVER SETTLE

They consistently do more than is expected of them and accept risk. They speak their mind on an issue, whether their view is popular or unpopular. The always strive to learn more, do more and be more, even if this means being single for a while. Their work ethics demand the best and accept nothing less.

Let's review some quotes from successful leaders in their fields about their thoughts on "being uncomfortable":

The truth is that our finest moments are most likely to occur when we are feeling deeply uncomfortable, unhappy, or unfulfilled. For it is only in such moments, propelled by our discomfort, that we are likely to step out of our ruts and start searching for different ways or truer answers.
~M. Scott Peck (Psychiatrist)

You have to dream it before you can achieve it. Be bold and audacious in setting goals. Get comfortable with being uncomfortable, define the barriers, craft a plan, and get on with the journey.
~Kenneth H. Shields (Salesman)

To make the individual uncomfortable, that is my task.
~Friedrich Nietzsche (Philosopher)

Comfort feels nice but does not foster growth.
~James Michael Lafferty (CEO)

I think goals should never be easy; they should force you to work, even if they are uncomfortable at the time.
~Michael Phelps (Olympian)

I have found that this willingness to embark on new experiences, often uncertain, sometimes uncomfortable, and even a bit frightening, is key to growth. This has become clearer and clearer to me as the years have gone by.
~John E. Pepper (Businessman)

chapter one

CEO Leadership Actions

1.1   Think briefly about yourself and other leaders in your leadership team and consider how well you reflect the virtues of an uncomfortable CEO.

1.2   Discuss your findings with your leadership team. Create a list of expectations to shape the new virtues.

chapter two

Today's Paradigm Shifts to Assess IT Priorities

Contradictions do not exist.
Whenever you think you are facing a contradiction,
check your premises. You will find that one of them is wrong.
~Ayn Rand–Atlas Shrugged

This chapter discusses the most critical paradigm shifts that any business' IT organization is coping with in the twenty-first century. You may be wondering if this will be about IT buzz words. Not at all! I will focus on five key paradigm shifts that are of the utmost importance, and perhaps unknown to you:

1. Outpacing the competition

2. IT belongs at the strategic table

3. Above and beyond IT cost control

4. From IT risk to IT contribution

5. The CIO's leadership role

The paradigm shifts aren't inhibiting your company's performance but a failure to recognize and embrace them might be. This chapter not only explains the shifts, but also provides suggestions on how to embrace and benefit from them.

First of all, let's discuss an existing perception about dealing with information technology in the business. Why do IT organizations have such a difficult time supporting rapidly changing businesses? And why does the problem seem to be getting worse, not better? Some would have you believe that it may be an insurmountable task. Why? Here are four anecdotal facts:

1. More than half of all the capital expenses incurred by businesses worldwide go to IT. However, most of the senior executives and boards remain skeptical as to whether their IT investments are paying off. (2.4)

2. According to a recent Oliver Wyman analysis (2.2), the world's 500 largest companies lose more than **$14 billion** every year because of failed IT projects.

3. According to a large-scale research of 5,400 IT projects conducted jointly in 2012 by McKinsey and the University of Oxford (2.3), it was found that 17 percent of them went so badly that they could threaten the very existence of the company.

4. According to a Gartner report (2.5), two-thirds of the CEOs hope that information technology will make a greater strategic value contribution to their industries in the future. However, they also believe that the core leadership capability their CIOs must address is that deep business understanding is the most serious shortfall.

Therein lies an opportunity!

Everyone understands there are business benefits, right? The problem is that executives and board directors are too busy and do not see the value in working with the CIO on alternatives to improve IT performance because of stories like the above described.

My commitment is that through this book, I will show you that when IT is fully engaged and leveraged, a business should experience a step-change improvement in incremental value (i.e., revenue growth, operating margin, asset efficiency and IT risk management). I will also discuss how to become more closely connected with your CIO, and the role information technology plays in equipping your company with relevance, speed and innovation.

Paradigm #1: Outpacing the Competition

Since the time of Adam Smith (1723–1790), two common business notions have shaped the essence of the capitalist model. Companies have worked hard on managing and improving two critical flows:

1. Products/services

2. Revenue drivers across the value chain

They constantly rethink and redesign ways to outperform their competition and reinvent new ways to manage the flow of products/services and revenue across the value chain so that they become better, faster and ultimately report profit and gains back to their shareholders. However, as the twenty-first century unfolds, that approach may not suffice to outpace competition. Leading companies all over the world have shown us that perhaps the only possible way to win in the marketplace is by maximizing another flow…I will call this additional flow the "third flow mandate:"

3. Shared information.

Shared information has become as important as the products/services and the revenue drivers themselves. Information is critical to performing any task or making any decision, and sharing information about what is relevant to your trading partners (i.e., clients, suppliers and consumers) is a must. But the real business success takes place only when you have the ability to jointly create, capture, and then commercialize value along with your trading partners. This can only be achieved if business information is shared effectively and consistently among all involved parties. The third flow becomes a catalyzer to enhance and improve the other two flows. It is the source of business insight and a means of business collaboration (i.e., the "glue" that holds products, services, revenue, and all partners together, all elements organized for collaboration).

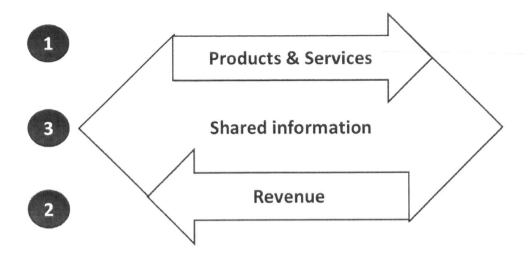

In the twenty-first century, the multi-directional flow of shared information binds and advances key business objectives.

To accomplish your company's mission and better serve your customers, you must foster collaboration with your trading partners. For example, if your company is a telecommunications services firm, your mission might state, "We develop world-class telecommunications products and services for our business and consumer markets through shared solutions to key strategic and operational issues with our trading partners." This implicitly recognizes the strategic value of the third flow.

Your business information—as the most strategic asset—should allow you to:

- Find operational efficiencies;
- Identify new market opportunities, and;
- Gain insight to uncover hidden patterns of consumer behavior and previously unrecognized correlations.

I will briefly share two practical examples from the two of the largest global retailers—Walmart (USA) and Tesco (UK)—and how they launched a truly revolutionary concept two decades ago: a capability to build closer and stronger relationships with their suppliers, knowing what their shoppers like and become sensitive to what they need.

Retail Link® (from Walmart) shares key business data such as: 1) store sales trends, 2) new items performance, 3) inventory levels and, more importantly, 4) consumer basket size averages. This concept continues to be a pioneering approach as it enhances and accelerates operational efficiency by making data-driven (i.e., third flow) decisions easy. How does it work? Once a company becomes an approved Walmart supplier, not only does it get free access to the Retail Link®, but it also receives training and guidance in how to use Retail Link® with confidence as a crucial means to its business success with Walmart!

The Shop® (from Tesco) shares key business data such as identifying: 1) shopper trends, 2) shopping basket patterns, 3) cross-selling, and 4) drivers to increasing store visits. Contrary to popular belief, Tesco's most significant competitive advantage is not scale, but rather knowledge. According to Tesco's CEO, Sir Terry Leahy, Tesco is big because it is good, not vice versa.

The value of the third flow as a means to drive business collaboration with trading partners creates opportunities to leverage these relationships in a more strategic and focused manner that delivers your company mission. Back in the mid-1990s, P&G embarked on a global sales restructure to transform the entire sales organization, from a pure "sales-only" silo into a rather multifunctional team approach with staffing from sales, marketing, supply chain, IT, logistics, finance and human resources. Most of the new teams were collocated closer to P&G's key retailers; their mission was revamped to deliver the retailer value equation and jointly work with the key retailers on agreed joint objectives. In other words, they implemented a third flow plan to strengthen a deeper consumer understanding. This model has been consolidated and currently, P&G has a similar approach to work with all customers and channels.

Let's talk now about the business challenges with the quality of your internal data sources if you decide to embark onto a third flow journey. One of the biggest obstacles you will find is with the quality of your business data. Unless you have a sound and well-articulated strategy and data governance model, it is very unlikely that your business data is ready and available to go outside your own company boundaries. In some cases, each function (finance, sales, demand planning, marketing, logistics, etc.) has created and used multiple definitions and representations of the same concept (e.g. customer, brand, employee), and even stored them in different and fragmented systems. These limitations about data management restrict the ability to respond swiftly to competitive changes in the business and constrain the ability to execute strategic plans.

In a world of financial uncertainty, constantly growing competition, worldwide Internet usage and increased regulation, the focus on standardizing (and optimizing) the third flow is a fundamental requirement to compete, protect and deliver results, as well as to derive incredible insights and create a huge competitive advantage.

The Scope and Direction of Internet Use

Internet growth has been exponential, with profound changes to how people consume information and how information is disseminated. The following statistics provide a glimpse into the information age we all live in:

- More than 2.4 billion people use the Internet. (2.6)

- There are some 660 million web pages, and Google has indexed more than a trillion pages. (2.6)

- The annual growth in data shared and stored and the number of Internet requests processed is 58 percent, or 5,800 percent over ten years. (2.6)

- 10% of all Internet traffic is on mobile devices. (2.6)

- If a single star is a bit of information, there's a galaxy of information for every person in the world. However it is still less than 1 percent of the information stored in all the DNA molecules of a human being. (2.6)

- The scope can be overwhelming. As Eric Schmidt, Google executive chairman, has pointed out, "Today, we produce more information at a higher speed than ever before. We create as much information in two days now as we did from the dawn of man through 2003." (August 4, 2010) (2.8)

- According to the Nielsen Company, the global average time spent per person on social networking sites is now nearly 5.5 hours per month. (February 2010)

What kinds of information is being created and consumed? The following figure shows examples of the amounts and types of information being created or consumed per minute.

Information Created Every Minute (June 2012–Domo Inc.) (2.8)

Has your executive leadership team discussed this situation? Perhaps you and your CIO should lay the foundation for a company-wide intervention to address potential gaps in your current data, standards, processes, and information systems. One key deliverable may be to ensure that all relevant stakeholders in the organization and in partner organizations have access to the same business rules for data. The overarching goal is to ensure the ability to deliver a single source of reference with harmonized, accurate and smartly managed stored critical business data.

This may undoubtedly be the very basic and core foundation capability in your IT portfolio.

Paradigm #2: IT Belongs at the Strategic Table

While some companies have kept pace with the transformations mentioned above, it is very unfortunate to see quite a few CIOs—or even worse, entire IT organizations—being isolated and disconnected from the rest of the company. In some cases, it seems as if the IT organization is a "company within the company," with its own culture, norms, and priorities. Four patterns clearly describe frequent attitudes and behaviors, as well as the opportunities involved:

1. IT has not earned a seat at the strategic table. In other words, IT is nothing more than just another commodity service provider like water and electricity. This notion was made widely popular by Nicholas G. Carr. (2.9) Many executives find that IT leaders are not capable of leading a good business discussion, and this is the most serious shortfall.

2. Board governance and executive coaching are almost non-existent in the area of information technology. IT governance is often delegated to the audit committee.

3. Maintain the annual IT budget down to the bare minimum. However, contrary to popular belief, the real issue is not the budget, but rather the lack of communication and understanding! A CIO who can clearly articulate the business value of IT can better establish stronger and lasting relationships (i.e., building bridges) between IT and other disciplines, including the board and its executive team.

4. Many business leaders recognize that their organizations use some type of "shadow IT systems" distinct from the company IT. Business employees (i.e. sales, supply chain, finance, marketing,

etc.) use that because they think there is no other way to get the work done, or to find the data and/or solutions they need to run their specific roles. Make no mistake, this is a very complex problem that may create additional and non-intended situations, such as:

- First of all, it blurs—or even worse, inhibits—the tracing mechanism established by stricter financial laws similar to Sarbanes-Oxley (SOX) in the USA, (or other laws in Europe, Japan and Australia) where public companies must trace key data flows that end up in the financial statements.

- Scary statistic: A very substantive portion of overall IT expenditure is unplanned around quick fixes with long lasting cost impacts and managed by the business community, circumventing the IT corporate governance. Gartner predicts that by 2015, "35% of enterprise IT expenditures will occur outside of the corporate IT budget. Employees will regularly subscribe to collaboration, analytic and other services they want, all with the press of a button." (2.10)

- Company-wide systems integration, data storage, analytics and data services to customers cannot evolve without better IT collaboration. This situation compromises the third flow.

Paradigm #3: Above and Beyond IT Cost Control

The basic purpose of IT management is to ensure an adequate supply of resources to support the development and maintenance of the IT platform and the new projects approved in the pipeline. The real opportunity is not in project cost controls but instead, in project scope creeping.

A clever, albeit intense, way to maintain control over project cost is to establish strong top management accountability to approve project scope changes (and their impact on incremental project costs). Allowing scope creeping without the proper scope management oversight will lead to the usage of incremental resources and create the need for additional timing.

Multiple techniques and management routines have been designed for the purpose of improving cost and scope management. At least, these should yield an improved IT performance.

Once you have solved the very basic challenge of getting your IT cost structure under control, you should ask yourself what the next performance level for IT should be.

Information technology should be considered a strategic resource to *transform* the business model, to *enable* decision making and to *co-lead* business innovation. Perhaps you are beginning to feel a bit uncomfortable with the last paragraph. You may find yourself thinking that transforming, enabling and co-leading business innovation does not sound like something that IT should or indeed can do.

This is a good opportunity to share a brief consulting experience. Some years ago, I presented these same three elements (transform, enable, co-lead) to the recently appointed CEO "John X."

> Before assuming his new role, John X. was a very successful chief marketing officer in a global company. He was my newly appointed business boss and it was our first business meeting to capture ideas for the new annual strategic plan. We actively engaged in the conversation about the new role of IT and what his specific expectations would be. During the conversation, we talked about business challenges and opportunities to better serve the retailers and also to improve the operation through a faster distribution network. He especially enjoyed my ideas about redesigning the supply

chain capability using a demand signal from our key clients to reduce the time-to-market by two or three days. I also talked about creating an executive cockpit from which the executive leadership team and all of the operations VPs would be able to steer the business in real time.

And lastly, once I felt that the meeting had gone very smoothly, I suggested, "John, the final element is that I would like to offer you my two best IT leaders to help co-lead the company's innovation taskforce."

I initially expected he would be pleased with my third idea, but I was sadly mistaken. His immediate response was: "No way! Innovation is not for IT people. Your people work on technical stuff, but not on the consumer interface. Innovation is a company capability solely owned by marketing, sales and product development. Thanks, but no thanks."

Clearly, his initial response was a logical one drawn from twenty-five-plus years of working experience; he was obviously not used to having an IT leader team actively engaged in innovation activities. The good news is that after a couple of cups of coffee and a few more minutes of open and candid discussion, I was able to convince him that as the new CEO, he might be looking for a lot more openness ahead and want to establish good expectations about collaboration and creativity among all of his employees. He finally agreed to assign my two IT leaders to the innovation task force. I left his office with the satisfaction of having helped the new CEO with three creative ideas for the annual business plan (transform, enable and co-lead).

Unfortunately, the situation described above is not unique. According to a 2012 study conducted by CA Technologies (2.12), 34 percent of the respondents among the 800 global business and IT executives surveyed characterize their relationship with IT as combative, distrustful or isolated, and only 21 percent of business executives identified IT as an "authority or expert" on innovation.

The traditional approach where IT should optimize and excel with the company's resources (i.e., minimize cost of acquisition, software/hardware maintenance and development) is important but not sufficient for the future.

My recommendation is a radical one. It is rooted in a critical condition: What can you expect IT to do for your business? Which function can be better equipped than information technology to respond with relevance and speed to the business demands in the so-called Connected Era? Applying a business perspective with a focus on systemic thinking and IT value-creation yield significant competitive advantages.

Furthermore, perhaps, your IT organization is already capable and eager to address specific business problems or opportunities (i.e., applying IT data analytics for a marketing shopper research or leveraging IT project management "know-how" to a large company project). Give them a good opportunity to increase their scope and reach.

To do so, the three essential elements introduced previously are necessary: transform, enable, and co-lead.

1) **Transform** the business model (i.e., company's strategies, operation and growth) by freeing up capacity for innovation, by improving efficiency, managing complexity, and reducing costs.

2) **Enable** the executive decision-making process with concise, decisive, multi-focused, real-time data streams solutions, by providing the executive leadership team with adequate tools to analyze business patterns in an effective way.

3) **Co-lead** the innovation process using the most effective collaboration and relationship capabilities, by getting new

products and services out more rapidly, or expanding into new geographies and markets.

More to discuss about these three essential elements in
Chapter Four: Success Criteria Lead to Success

Paradigm #4: From IT Risk to IT Contribution

Unfortunately, many CEOs and board directors are disappointed with their CIOs' ability to drive IT business value. A large portion of the boards think of IT as a commodity. They are more concerned with the highest liabilities such as major/expensive projects, data security, cyber-attacks, and risks compromising the third flow (shared information). They are also vocal about the fact that their CIOs simply cannot get a true grasp on the IT business value for the corporation they serve. More than half of the boards delegate the responsibility of IT oversight to the audit committee.

It is obvious that defining, measuring and maximizing the IT business value remains elusive to most companies. Based on my consulting experience, I have seen three different board actions with regards to the IT agenda. First of all, they invest some extra time to oversee IT's performance and to understand the risks and potential exposure. The CIO owns an agenda item to report all the key IT issues and the mitigation plans in place. Secondly, in very few companies, they trust and empower their internal IT organization. The CIO maintains and improves performance while appropriately addressing key IT issues. And the third action, representing a new and emerging trend, some boards have included an external CIO or an IT executive consultant as part of the board structure. This may be a good way, ensuring proper alignment of business and IT strategy while having a voice that can contribute as an independent point of view.

Each of the three actions serves important, yet very narrow objectives (risk management, issues management, and external oversight). All are missing a key element. Let's briefly review that.

We now live in a super-connected world economy—products are sold across borders; communication is instantaneous and global; inventory production schedules are inextricably linked; the shopper-centric marketing process is becoming the norm. In this new context, the real key question is how the CIO should increase the CEO and the board's awareness beyond "IT risks & oversight," to "IT contribution" and its impact, freeing up capacity for innovation, improving efficiency, managing complexity and reducing costs. In other words, how the CIO should help you with the company's strategies, operation and growth. This is something that merits serious discussion between you and your CIO.

The real issue the CIO needs to discuss with the CEO and board

Paradigm #5: CIO Leadership Role

New leadership traits that differentiate successful CIOs from average CIOs are on the rise. The way businesses operate now is quite challenging and different. First of all, let's describe the current business environment: there are rapid technological changes, increased worldwide connections, population growth, and income disparities; knowledge has become an important asset and, more importantly, there is a new workforce generation known as "digital natives." (2.13) (For example, university students who have spent their entire lives surrounded by and using computers, video games, digital music players, video cams, cell phones, and all the other toys and tools of the digital age.)

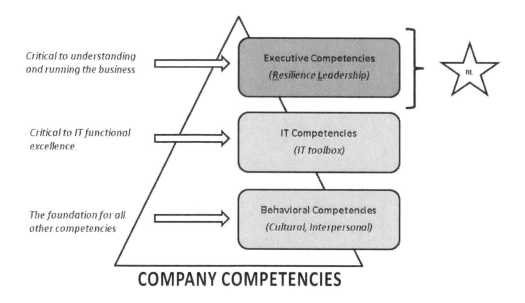

Resilient Leadership Competencies (2.11)

It is taken for granted that the CIOs must be competent and knowledgeable about behavioral competencies and also about IT as "a toolbox;" their technical skill sets must be consistently sharpened and their technology background must be constantly updated with new methods and technologies. But there is something else that sets them apart, something about how to lead from the front, instead of from the rear. For the CIOs to be successful, above all else, they need to learn and practice resilient leadership.

If you Google "resilient Leadership," you will find more than 7 million different hits. Let's narrow it down to the eight key attributes:

1. Sets a winning direction. Success is contagious.
2. Copes with stress and adversity.
3. Takes risks with confidence in achieving the best results.
4. Listens and communicates with transparency.
5. Translates internal collaboration and external competition into actions.

6. Never settles for less than the best of the vision.
7. Is not about doing one specific thing very well, but rather about flexibility and diversity of thought.
8. Demonstrates sustained competence exhibited by individuals who experience challenging conditions.

Since success is contagious, one success will often lead to another, and one successful person will influence another to be successful. The job of a resilient CIO is to start the fire that fuels the virtuous cycle of success. A resilient CIO is a leader who has a strong purpose in life, consistently manages ambiguity while making informed and timely decisions, and yet has the ability to bounce back in the face of adversity. A resilient CIO dares to take far-reaching, informed risks and shows confidence in achieving best results, both at the business and the organizational level, and lastly, never settles for less than the best of the agreed-to vision. He or she must leverage experiences from the past, minimize corporate risks, stay alert to the technological pace and establish a solid connection between information technology and the company's goals. IT organizations under the lead of a resilient CIO know how to listen and communicate well, they understand how to collaborate with other functions and colleagues, and they demonstrate strong and ethical competition in the marketplace. Lastly, they build their success one step at a time, always aiming for winning results from start to finish.

Keeping up with those five paradigms shifts at the core of this chapter and combining them with the key tenets of resilient leadership is an extremely difficult task for any CIO.

That has to change.

Since the 2008 financial crisis, many boards have reviewed the executive compensation plans to ensure the alignment of pay and performance. Without getting into specifics, this implies that companies need to make organizational commitments to changing the role of the CIO and define CIO objectives to encourage operating radically differently and help the business growth with sustainable and scalable solutions. Now more than ever before, CEOs and board directors need for the CIOs to perform as "advisors" using good business acumen and with the ability to navigate in a rapidly changing global environment.

For perspective, a Fortune 10 company has recently added the following "CEO guidelines" into its formal top management training program:

- Information technology is changing the business landscape. We all know this is so, because we all use the Internet.

- Information technology can be a catalyst to facilitate important work process change.

- To be effective, information technology people must be plugged in and given the broadest possible scope in our business.

- However, an effective information technology and business interface is a two-way street: Strengthening the IT-business liaison role must be combined with driving greater business partner capability and accountability.

What happens when the CIO embraces the new expectations and provides a set of actions to address the five aforementioned paradigms? Significant assistance is provided to the CEO and to the board in responding to the complexity of increasingly interconnected organizations, markets, and consumers in four specific areas:

1. Aligning IT goals with the corporate needs and objectives.

2. Operating as the primary agent of change with more seamless project adoption results and minimal risks.

3. Performing lead work closely with key stakeholders to ensure that IT initiatives provide substantial benefit to core business functions.

4. Fostering a corporate culture of collaboration and relationships, essential to fueling innovation.

chapter two

CEO LEADERSHIP ACTIONS

2.1   Increase and improve quality time with your CIO. Try to understand first. Your CIO will be initially pleased with the opportunity to talk to you about his or her functional responsibilities.

2.2   Discuss with your board organizational commitments to changing the role of the CIO and define CIO objectives to encourage operating "radically differently."

2.3   Discuss with your CIO plans for the board to become digitally literate and help them to understand how IT is paramount in gaining competitive advantage.

2.4   Discuss with your CIO plans for the board to become digitally literate, and help them to understand how IT is paramount in gaining competitive advantage.

2.5   Explore ideas with your CIO to change the conversation from "IT risk" to "IT contribution." What needs to be done?

chapter three

REFLECTIONS ON VALUE

A rule of thumb: *Until a value-creation model (VCM) becomes*
an integral part of the way a company manages information technology,
it will always be merely "something else to do" and will inevitably fail
as employees continue to perform as they always have.
Finance department input is essential, for example, but delegating VCM
to the finance department as a discrete, isolated program is a surefire way
to snuff its potential.
~A. G. Lafley

At the outset of this chapter, here are three very basic definitions of *value*:

- According to Merriam-Webster, value means: *a fair return or equivalent in goods, services or money for something exchanged, something intrinsically desirable. To value is to set priorities, to assign meaning and richness of properties to reality. It is to choose one thing over another. It is to think about things in relation to each other and decide that one is better than the other.* In reality, value, in modern terms, means not only money, or material or exchange worth—it is about living better lives in a better world! It is defined by the beholder.

- Professor Durward Hofler (Northeastern Illinois University) often teaches his students—myself included—that "value and values are not the same." He says, "Values are specific items that people stand for, believe in, or deem important. Values bind people together as an organization. Values contribute to the creation of an environment where people can be at their best; representing people's most significant commitment to what they find most important in life."

- Shareholder value: The key goal of most companies is to increase wealth creating monetary value for their shareholders. In layman's terms, the shareholders' money should yield a return that is commensurate with the risk in similar industries.

However, it is quite difficult for most of the employees to verify that their work priorities are building "shareholder value." For perspective, how could you determine if a given IT system is actually building or eroding shareholder value? Most companies have broken shareholder value down into four key value drivers to track sustained performance and growth:

1. **Revenue Growth**: Growth in the company's "top line" in exchange for products and services.

2. **Operating Margin (after tax)**: The portion of revenue that is left over after taxes and the costs of providing products and services.

3. **Investment (Assets) Efficiency**: A company that generates more revenue from fewer assets is more efficient than one that requires huge assets to generate the same revenue.

4. **Execution Capabilities**: The confidence the marketplace has in the company's ability to perform well in the future. The key elements include the board's governance, the talent of the company's people, its go-to-market execution capabilities, and its market leadership and innovation.

As intuitive as these financial principles may sound, very few companies actually put them into practice to value the information technology contribution.

David Walters (3.1) cites Adam Smith's notion of "value-in-use." Smith's idea, introduced in 1776, was that the end user should consider all aspects of a product-service purchase, not simply the price paid, enabling both vendors and purchasers to identify all of the elements of the procurement: installation, operation, maintenance, and replacement continuum. Furthermore, Walters explained that value-in-use is the perceived value that is available to the customer/consumer when considering a purchase. Use value is a subjective assessment of the benefits available (the consumer surplus and the price actually negotiated with the vendor of the price/service). If we assume price and value-in-use to be the consumer-choice criteria, we approach a commercially acceptable definition of value-in-use.

Value-In-Use

When considering value and information technology, it is useful to think of value in two senses:

- **Asset value:** includes hardware, software, IT's organization processes and skills. This is relatively easy to estimate but normally yields lower value because it considers standard practices.

- **Value-in-use**: business value from IT is of economic and/or strategic value depending on business priorities. This is fairly complex to estimate but yields higher value.

Traditionally the CIO's primary responsibility is to employ standard practices and performance measures in order to track IT's *asset value*. Developing *value-in-use* requires a different mindset. The CIO must identify new levers and their intersection with other functions and disciplines. For instance, the CIO could explore *value-in-use* using the following business priorities: 1) operational excellence, 2) procurement and sourcing, 3) security and risk management, 4) operational planning and 5) go-to-market initiatives.

Value-in-use is different for each company, each industry segment and even each key stakeholder. In other words, information technology may bring value to the commercial organization by reducing sales time or closing deals more quickly, to the finance organization by improving cash flow, to the supply chain by improving customer service satisfaction, and so on.

We cannot figure out how to get to where we want to go unless we understand where we are right now. Critical to measuring value-in-use is to determine where the company will be in the near future as well as how to get there. One task companies often carry out when deploying their strategic plans is to prepare a detailed analysis about leadership accountability versus performance metrics. This requires close alignment between the individual or team goals and performance metrics for the company to achieve its strategic plan.

Case Study: A Culture of IT Value-Creation

Let's describe how the P&G IT organization implemented a "value-in-use" model. (3.2) In a world that continues to accelerate faster than ever before, P&G top management realized the value provided by the IT organization and encouraged IT to find new and better ways to make and use information and technology solutions as a competitive advantage in the marketplace. Add to this the challenge of delivering quality services at continually declining costs—all the while supporting increasing demand for such services—and you will understand the need to rethink the way IT had to reinvent itself.

With the support of A. G. Lafley (CEO of P&G), the following three-element plan was crafted:

1. Development of best-of-breed partnerships across the globe— including companies such as HP and IBM—to deliver services and ensure operational excellence.

2. Categorization of services based on the way employees and business leaders consume and use them. And lastly,

3. Development of business relevant value-in-use criteria to work across the entire company.

By 2005, Procter & Gamble communicated a new way to improve IT services and solutions to its entire employee community; it was branded as "*Running IT as a Business.*" Along the way, the company identified three elements for successfully making the shift to the entirely new IT "value-in-use" mindset. The goal was to identify how to do the right work more efficiently. By simplifying the way IT employees work together and communicate plans, IT should free up resources to manage increased demand for services and to focus on work that will deliver the greatest *value-in-use.*

First, management must encourage the new IT solutions to bring a better total user experience; in other words, success should be based on how the end users (in this instance, the employees) perceived the new IT solutions. Management had to anticipate some reluctant IT leaders and prepare them to make the shift from technical consultant to full business partner.

Second, management needs to ensure that the design of the IT organization reflects and reinforces the end user-centric focus. This led to the adoption of service levels and the value creation model. This allowed IT to implement several service managers in charge of providing the adequate service to different stakeholders throughout the company. For example, P&G staffed full-time IT teams dedicated to support supply, sales, finance, and marketing service-oriented solutions.

And third, management must create a sustainable model where cost is optimized. Helping improve P&G's productivity is why "*Running IT as a Business*" was branded and cost savings is an important component of that. It focuses on understanding the needs of clients and users, and helps IT deliver against those needs with excellence. But it was also about simplifying the IT structure and the business work processes so management could free up capacity for more meaningful work. By being able to focus on what is most important, IT has delivered even better results at lower costs and continues to control its own future.

P&G ⬌	Information Technology
Consumer Benefits	Total User Experience
Market Share	Service Levels
Volume	Value-creation
Brand Management	Service Management
Profit/Loss	Cost

"Running IT as a Business"—P&G (2005)

If there is a mismatch between the target and the results, the organization will underperform—certain pockets of employees (or even entire functions) will have "blind spots" with respect to the company's goals. Anticipating those blind spots is an extremely critical responsibility for the CIO when it comes to driving broad business support and implementing new solutions in the marketplace. In contrast, if there is an excellent match, the organization will recognize the utmost importance of the strategic plan and will do whatever is necessary to align and promote cooperation across the entire company.

The pursuit of value-in-use enables the IT organization to become a true strategic partner for the company by creating business solutions and solving business problems effectively. Let's look at six specific areas that are useful in driving a culture of IT value-creation:

1. Align strategy with vision. Walk the talk (align words with actions).

2. Ensure that all moving parts are in sequence.

3. Clarify roles and integrate them with clear individual/team performance metrics.

4. Confirm that the IT game plan (or project portfolio) is using value-in-use creation metrics.

5. Ensure that all key stakeholders have a clear understanding of the IT game plan.

6. Communicate the long term and show what success looks like (see Chapter Four: Success Criteria Lead to Success).

As mentioned above, the principles of value-creation may appear to be simple, but implementing them, especially in a large company, is a whole new ball game. "Nothing can come of nothing," William Shakespeare said. Results are the outcome of what people in the organization do—tasks, habits, norms, standards and practices. These are all elements of culture. In this sense, culture is not something that should be of interest only to social scientists and anthropologists; it is a critical variable that influences results and should be understood by every leader.

All of these problems can be solved, but it takes full alignment within the executive leadership team. Unfortunately, there is no magic formula. There is no "program of the year" to achieve this. It takes hard work, the routine and continuous repetition of simple things that contribute to value-creation. This involves executive-level responsibility for constantly renewing and capitalizing on key areas. Your executive leadership team really needs to understand how the company culture operates:

1. Attitudes towards formal strategies and goals;

2. Actual distribution of power and rewards;

3. Actual work that people do and/or do not do;

4. Other norms that explain how things do or do not get done.

The OP Model

Now let's discuss an excellent framework called Organizational Performance Model (OP Model) developed by D. P. Hanna. (3.3) This model could help you improve the performance of large and complex organizations. The work cited above offers possible starting points for those wishing to pursue the subject more in depth. However, I would like to focus this discussion on a specific section about organization assessment and information technology. My experience is that when well managed, this framework can create improved organizational performance and overall satisfaction.

There is an old saying that goes, "All organizations are perfectly designed to get the results they get!" This means that there is always a way in which an organization finds its point of equilibrium in terms of demands and available resources. The desired organizational change depends on appropriate design of the organization and its operations.

Hanna proposes:

1. All the organizational elements (Structure, Rewards, Tasks, Decision-making, People, and Information) are in balance or not, to achieve results. All of these elements are interrelated. A change in one will undoubtedly produce some changes in the others.

2. Culture is actually the result of the interaction between the six design elements. These design elements are what in reality determine the difference between what we say we will do (Strategy and Plans) and what we actually do (Culture).

An easy way to describe the complex interactions between the six organizational elements is provided by Hanna through the "perfect hexagon" analogy. Any given organization could be represented by a perfect hexagon with six symmetrical sides and six symmetrical vertices. The six symmetrical angles represent: people, rewards, information, tasks, structure, and decision-making.

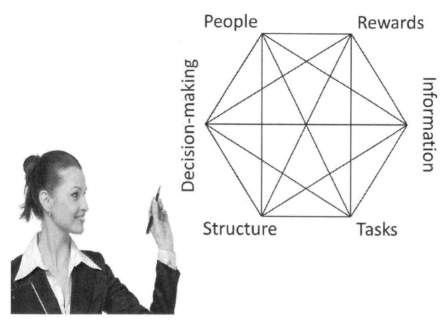

The OP Model Hexagon—Hanna (3.3)

As a corollary: whenever a new information technology solution is implemented in any organization, the project team must always complete a change assessment using the six organizational elements to verify whether the organization elements can embrace the changes to their full potential in harmony. To illustrate this, I will use the following example:

> The IT organization was chartered to develop a flexible system to handle the entire sales field merchandising cycles with the company's clients. The new system will produce statements as often as it is required without having to remember to "CLOSE THE BILLING PERIODS," or other complicated financial steps. The system was named as *MERCH-FAST*.

Reference to each one of the six organizational elements will be placed in parentheses for easier identification.

The *MERCH-FAST* implementation would change the way sales managers approve merchandising plans for their field salespeople (**INFORMATION**). With the new system, all of the merchandising plans will be approved much faster using an automated process with a complex algorithm to trace common patterns, validate price and marketing conditions and verify investment targets. The field sales teams believe that faster approvals will give them a good competitive advantage. However, they also feel that using a predefined business template is a bit too cumbersome; they will need now to fill in all the data fields (**TASKS**). According to some field users, the previous work process was much easier and very flexible since all they needed to do was to send a brief email requesting funds.

Furthermore, has the project team given a thought about what is the new job description for the sales managers? Before *MERCH-FAST,* the sales managers were responsible to approve all funds—one by one. In some cases they used to spend considerable daily hours on the approval process. Now with the new system what is going to happen to them? Should some sales managers be redeployed to work on other sales areas? (**STRUCTURE** & **PEOPLE**). *MERCH-FAST* will automatically approve all of the new funding merchandising plans. Does that mean that the sales manager will no longer be held accountable for his or her field sales teams' merchandising funding? What kind of tracking and supervision mechanism will be in place for the sales managers to lead their field teams effectively (**DECISION-MAKING**)? And lastly, how should top management drive the proper adoption to the new process, recognizing early adopters and coaching late users (**REWARDS**)?

As you have noted, there are quite a few important elements that could potentially derail the implementation of *MERCH-FAST* and eventually erode the IT value creation. Evidently, there is more than "just" building a new software when it comes to running IT solutions successfully. It is of critical relevance to keep an eye on all six organization elements when implementing any information technology solution.

In the following table, I describe three possible outcomes for the implementation of information technology solutions and the corresponding hexagons.

Three Possible Outcomes while Implementing IT Solutions

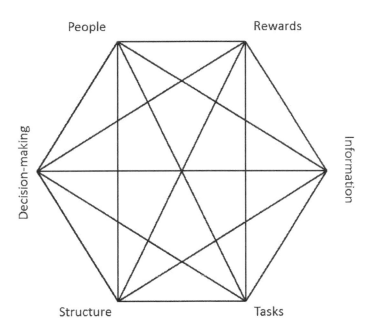

The six elements play the role and function for which the new solution was designed.

Organization in TRANSITION

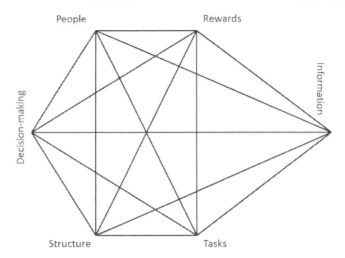

A new information solution is being implemented. The organization is under stress learning how to operate with the new set of data and all of the changes to its routine. Overall, there is a need to maintain a total balancing act for time, attention, resources, and energy. The project team needs to complete a full assessment to understand the impact of the new system.

Organization is UNBALANCED

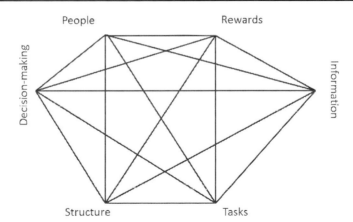

While adopting the new IT solution, the project team needs to be careful not to disturb what is working well now. Any change will probably have both good and bad connotations for whatever your current design and objectives are. The challenge is to come up with a new hexagon, perhaps different, faster, and more responsive, while preserving the essence of staying in equilibrium. In this example, the project team implemented the new solution, but was then disbanded, leaving an unbalanced organization with three uneven angles (People, Rewards, and Information). There is extra work to be done to bring the organization back into EQUILIBRIUM.

The practical value of the "OP Model" lies not only in its schematic depiction but also in understanding how the company culture actually operates and then comparing those results to the business requirements.

In closing, you and your CIO should be able to create value using information technology as a driver of strategic change. Do not expect any less.

Keep in mind that if your current company's mindset is prone to reverting to an "obsolete" state, where IT value-creation is just another buzz word or "a waste of the company's time," you need to take on the difficult task of developing a value-creation mentality—not as a temporary measure, but as a permanent way of operating. With your leadership and constant discipline, you and the executive team will institutionalize a good IT value-creation mindset.

chapter three

CEO LEADERSHIP ACTIONS

3.1   Analyze your current IT game plan (IT portfolio) in terms of the four key value drivers. Assign priorities based on the "best" value promised.

3.2   Explore one or two value-in-use metrics with your CIO. Is the value rendered worth the effort? What can you *stop, start, and continue?*

3.3   How effectively is your company driving a culture of IT value-creation? Qualify strengths and opportunities with the OP Model hexagon.

chapter four

SUCCESS CRITERIA LEAD TO SUCCESS

"Would you tell me, please, which way I ought to go from here?"
"That depends a good deal on where you want to get to," said the Cat.
"I don't much care where..." said Alice.
"Then it doesn't matter which way you go," said the Cat.
"...so long as I get somewhere," Alice added as an explanation.
"Oh, you're sure to do that," said the Cat, *"if you only walk long enough."*
"In that direction," the Cat said. *"They're both mad."*
"But I don't want to go among mad people," Alice remarked.
"Oh, you can't help that," said the Cat. *"We're all mad here. I'm mad. You're mad."*
"You must be," said the Cat, *"Or you wouldn't have come here."*
~Lewis Carroll—Alice in Wonderland

Success is critical to every single organization. Delivering successful results leads to evolution and progress. However, skepticism often arises when determining information technology success criteria. Who decides? What must be considered? Should results be measured now or in the future? Are metrics such as budget, time and specifications sufficient? How many elements should be considered? What is the right organizational culture to lead success? These are questions that always need to be clarified before you embark on a new information technology initiative. This chapter provides some thoughts on the meaning of success in its broadest definition—how to determine "balanced" success criteria for information technology projects—and introduces a new framework to elevate the IT organization to the next level in terms of expectations and equity awareness.

What Is Success After All?

When I think about success, I always remember my grandfather, Manuel. He was a quiet Basque businessman with few words, especially for the little kids. However, he was good at grasping the essential ideas in life. Once he told me, "José Ignacio, as you become an adult, always remember that success is the accomplishment of a dream with a finite time and favorable outcomes." Sir Winston Churchill used to suggest that "Success is going from failure to failure without a loss of enthusiasm." Anyway, success is basically benchmarking.

The Iron Triangle

During the late 1950s, the first commercial computers (UNIVAC and IBM) hit the marketplace and became accessible mainly to academic researchers who shaped and defined concrete and succinct information technology success criteria. They came up with three elements they deemed to be sufficiently comprehensive and named these elements the "Iron Triangle." (4.1)

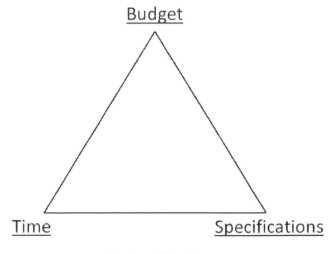

The Iron Triangle

It was believed then (as well as now) that meeting the following is a good definition of success for an information technology solution:

- Budget (how much it should cost)

- Time (when it must be built)

- Specifications (what must be built)

This was a very IT-centric model; not surprisingly, this definition was easily adopted throughout the entire industry and soon became the norm.

However, during recent decades, there has been an increase of highly sophisticated information technology solutions to support company-wide work processes, the globalization of business operations, mergers and acquisitions, almost real-time processing—all of the elements from our super-connected world economy. As expected, hardware, software, and telecommunication have grown accordingly. While all of the above has happened, we have not seen the same type of evolution for improved information technology success criteria. The majority of the project teams continue to apply almost the identical version of the Iron Triangle.

The fundamental challenges observed in today's business are twofold:

1. There are other key considerations that are not considered part of the Iron Triangle. They include: connectivity, productivity, flexibility, and above all, quality.

2. Key stakeholder groups may have different and perhaps conflicting priorities toward the approval of the new project success criteria.

Let's illustrate this with a brief example. During the stages of a project's life cycle—discovering, designing, building, and implementing—the project team has learned and realized that some of the initial project assumptions need to be revisited. Those new assumptions are very important for the end-user community. This implies a change of scope and very likely the need for extra resources to execute those changes. If the project team tries to deliver under the initial constraints, they will face key paradigms such as what is more important: the original budget, the committed timing, or the newly "discovered" specifications? Should they negotiate back with the stakeholders, explaining what they have found, or sacrifice the quality of the delivery? In the end, they feel that they are all of a sudden in a lose-lose situation. If the project team delivers at all, the quality of the delivered solution suffers and the project is most likely late and over budget.

Below are some other situations you may have already heard in your organization:

- Projects rated as "true disasters" because they were over budget and ran into long delays. However, the executive leadership team (and the end users) loved the final solutions and continue to use them in production, yielding incremental value to the company.

- Projects rated as "success" because they truly met the agreed Iron Triangle criteria. However, the user community did not use the given solution, as it became obsolete due to sudden or new changes in the requirements (i.e., imagine a recently implemented financial system immediately after the tax authorities approved new regulations).

- Of course, many information technology projects deliver successful and good results according to the Iron Triangle, but there also some projects that were approved, budgeted, designed, and even implemented without any success criteria ever having been defined.

What do you think about those situations? In any case, there is a need for a better, more realistic approach. The Iron Triangle is not sufficient to deal with today's business needs.

Project and Delivery Success

Before I define the new success criteria, it is important to differentiate between the terms "project success" and "delivery success."

The project success ("*get it right*") must be expressed in terms of the quality of value-in-use:

1. What is the business value-in-use delivered when the project is adopted? In other words, are projects always adopted in the organization to meet the business specifications?

2. The project should deliver business value-in-use during a pre-identified and reasonable future horizon. Responding to unanticipated requirements requires a certain flexibility that must be considered as part of the solution design.

This measures the value of your new IT solutions!

The delivery success of a project ("*do it right*") is measured by constraints or in-process metrics, but these are NOT project goals. Obviously, specifications, budget and timing are extremely relevant constraints, since they establish circumstances and operation boundaries that should be followed by the project team.

This measures the efficiency of your IT project delivery team!

The project success and the delivery success serve two potentially different stakeholder communities and different sets of requirements. Once conflicts arise, the CIO must assign priorities and a set of corrective actions. Recommendations for a balanced success criteria will be:

*   Create a "project champion" business role and use this to market the project and help serve as a conduit for ensuring appropriate stakeholder engagement throughout the life of the project.

- Conduct periodic audits of the integrated project.

- Develop a governance structure to assess the quality of IT projects.

Doing More with Less

With today's emphasis on getting MORE with LESS, your CIO and project teams should be accountable for improving project success rates AND for implementing standard delivery practices throughout the company.

Tarek Farahat, president of Latin America P&G, described this principle best:

> Average performers deliver MORE with MORE. You give them more money—they give you more business…you give more people—you get more work done. They deliver what is expected. Their mind is programmed in a mathematical way: MORE results are correlated with MORE people… money…time etc. Most organizations are full of average performers. You give them a goal; they come back with the list of requirements to deliver. If you do not meet the list, you do not get the work. They put the monkey back on you. No surprise in the relationship, you get what you pay for. I view these people as average performers. I continuously try to replace them with others from the MORE with LESS group. It is a better investment for my time and money. (4.2)

There are three key things we can keep in mind to ensure that we are equipped and protected in spite of these uncertain times:

1. The "balanced" success criteria are much broader, incorporating favorable value for all stakeholders in the project life cycle:

a) **Quality business value-in-use**: present and future

b) **Constraints**: specifications, budget, and time

2. According to Christopher Meyer, "the overarching purpose of success criteria should be to help the team, rather than the senior managers. Your project teams should be empowered to design their own measurement system." (4.3) If they cannot do that, you had better replace the project people with capable leaders.

3. For projects such as critical mission systems, quality (present and future) would be the overriding criteria. Make no mistake; the focus will be on "Get it right!" instead of "Do it right!" Of course, doing both would be great, but when it comes to setting expectations, your teams should know exactly what is important and what is nice to have. I echo Rodney Turner's comment at the International Journal of Project Management that "this is the art and science of converting vision into reality." (4.4)

	Project success	**Delivery success**
	Get it right!	Do it right!
Project life cycle	Quality business value-in-use <u>outcomes</u>: • Present • Future	Circumstances and operation <u>boundaries</u>: • Specs • Budget • Time
Community served	End users	Project delivery teams
What is measured?	How valuable are your new solutions?	How efficient is your project delivery team?

"Balanced" Success Criteria for Information Technology Projects

A New Framework to Elevate IT's Equity

We want IT to be measured on the
benefits delivered and value created.
As IT leaders we need to know which of our efforts are
creating value for the company and which are not;
and make sure our programs increase in value-creation year to year.
~A Leading Global CIO

Several years ago, I had the wonderful opportunity of attending a marketing strategy meeting with Vidal Sassoon. He was well known for his revolution of hairstyling, his TV commercials and for selling his company to the Procter & Gamble Company. At the meeting, he said something that still resonates with me: "The only place where success comes before work is in the dictionary." Bottom line, if any given IT organization wants to broaden its relevance of action beyond the technical boundaries and into the business area, they must work—work very smartly and even very differently.

In the following pages, I will articulate the characteristics of a *different* information technology organization using a *different* identity model through an example framework, wherein the identity model is the expression of an organization that is communicated to the outside world. It includes the organization's image, the affinities of its people, beliefs, voice, promises, and more. I argue that using this or a similar framework would elevate IT's equity and would help the CIO to course-correct the organization's plans discussed with the leadership team.

The overall goal is for IT to be easily recognized upon delivering a predefined, unique and distinctive promise to the key stakeholders. As you follow the example framework, keep in mind that successful organizations have the capacity to change before the case for the change becomes obvious.

Example Framework

- *You have just been appointed as the CIO of a mid-size global company.*

- *The status quo: The company's IT organization has been focused on providing cost-effective and scalable solutions to support internal and external go-to-market priorities.*

- *The forecast: The market potential is expected to double over the next five years via organic growth and important global acquisitions.*

- *The writing for a case of change is on the wall: the current IT solutions are highly fragmented and non-standard; they drain resources and slow down innovation; end users must perform significant manual work to capture and report "business" data.*

- *In short: This situation is not sustainable in the future. As it stands, the IT model follows a support strategy rather than a catalyst strategy.*

- *Your vision: A business-driven IT strategy can do more than just streamline the way data are accessed, shared and analyzed. The key is to demonstrate the joint value among the company, its customer's supply and demand activities. Ultimately, IT becomes the catalyst for change.*

You've assessed the situation, analyzed the challenges, and identified the desired outcome. Now what do you do? More importantly, how do you achieve it?

- *You share your assessment and plans for change with the CEO and the board. Your proposal is logical yet provocative, and minimizes risks very elegantly.*

- *Congratulations: You've successfully initiated the shift from passive (support strategy) to proactive (catalyst strategy). You got the board's approval.*

- *It's time to introduce the new identity model of the IT organization! You make the case for communicating the new model and the new mindset that underpins it to the entire company. The executive leadership team agrees to help you.*

- *In advance of communicating the new model to the entire company, you prepare the new IT identity model (keywords, visual elements and promises).*

The following table describes your creative work in this process—from co-leading innovation to establishing IT value:

Positioning Statement	
To:	Our company, where IT performs with a compelling interest to transform information into solutions for joint value-creation together with our stakeholders.
That:	Leads the delivery of market-driven business solutions and enables execution with excellence.
So:	The company is able to win in the marketplace and leverage our brands, products, and services by building sustainable and profitable growth.
Because:	IT brings a unique combination of deep business knowledge, project management, leadership, and a highly competitive drive.

Beliefs

Innovations: Creativity and risk-taking are part of our DNA, constantly challenging us to learn, allowing us to improve the way we execute and unlock new opportunities for business growth.

Sustainability: Streamlined and automated key business processes will efficiently enable business growth.

Collaboration: We are committed to working with our stakeholders and business partners to create unprecedented levels of business value.

Essence

- Transform the business

- Enable decision-making

- Co-lead innovation

- Establish innovative, scalable, sustainable solutions that drive profitable business growth for the company

Signposts

- Alignment with top management leadership groups

- New levels of transparency

- Opportunity to excel and develop new IT core competencies

- Personal accountability for career growth

Voice

The IT organization approaches problems with a 360° view of the company; we understand real-time business issues and translate them into innovative solutions that drive profitable, sustainable growth.

New Role

Define, measure, and increase IT value-creation.

Organization Success Criteria

1) **Partnerships:** To win in the marketplace, we focus our partnership efforts on and align our goals with the corporate needs, objectives, and the IT platform. We work closely with key stakeholders, internal as well as external, to ensure that IT initiatives provide substantial benefit to core business functions, as measured by increased revenue, net operating income and productivity.

2) **Strategic Focus:** Invest resources to eliminate non-core work. Drive alignment toward the company's mission. Ensure that the IT initiatives meet the organization's strategic goals. Provide a strategic direction to ensure that IT solutions are effectively utilized to drive the business efficiently. Install metrics and consistent processes to improve the overall benefits, using the IT solutions.

3) **Velocity:** Accelerating time-to-market is certainly one of the key reasons for success in today's economy. Our disciplined process encourages adaptation to manage changing business needs, teamwork, and accountability for rapid delivery of high-quality solutions.

4) **Frugality:** Services and solutions are scalable and reflect savings in how resources are applied to deliver affordable results at the best possible cost structure.

5) **Execution:** A bias for value-creation. Leading smart planning with discernment and judgment enables us to drive effective adoption throughout the company. We aim to hold ourselves and others accountable and inspire the organization by confronting issues and celebrating success.

IT Identity Model

- *Final steps: Your IT identity model and guidelines are completed. It is now time to launch them for the rest of the company. Think about how to capitalize on these options to include scheduling face-to-face sessions with all of your key stakeholder groups to explain the new IT approach and/or using a broadcast communication message followed by Q&A meetings.*

- *Prepare an effective launch and more importantly, walk the talk!*

- *We wish you success with your new IT identity model!*

There are two key things that we can keep in mind:

1. Reflect the five elements of the IT equity organization success criteria (*partnership, strategic focus, velocity, frugality, and execution*) in your CIO's annual leadership performance appraisal. This is a journey of knowledge, discipline, and business management. Leaders, including your CIO, must lead. As always, the real change starts at the top.

2. The "essence of IT" in your business should be well known by everybody in IT, as a constant reminder to the employees of why IT exists. I am a strong advocate of the three elements: Transform, Enable, and Co-lead.

chapter four

CEO Leadership Actions

4.1   Compare your existing project success criteria with the proposed "balanced" success criteria for IT projects. Make the necessary adjustments.

4.2   Privately coach your CIO on the variability of growth scenarios. If you need for IT to be more flexible, your company must be in a position to do better "what-if" planning.

4.3   Ask your CIO about the current IT identity model. It may be time to rethink the way IT operates; your CIO should come up with a new identity model. Suggest ideas to "put money to work." And publicly commend IT with the examples you appreciate.

4.4   Adjust your CIO and IT leadership team performance appraisals using the five-element IT equity organization success criteria.

chapter five

RESILIENCE IN AN UNCERTAIN MARKETPLACE

*As trade borders become seamless
and the world becomes more dependent on technology,
business executives must scramble to acquire the tools
and skills necessary to survive and thrive in the
increasingly competitive global market.*
~Mona Pearl—Grow Globally (5.1)

In this chapter, I will discuss those characteristics that most clearly and consistently define doing business in the twenty-first century: marketplace uncertainty, resilience, and talent. Of course, these characteristics are not always fully present at any given moment; but successful business leaders approach them in a very consistent way.

Uncomfortable CEOs face reality and have the courage to act. In the short term, this means making hard decisions that are never pleasant or popular. But these CEOs are willing to take steps that will make the organization better, even though they may be painful or even scary. In today's world, almost all businesses, in all industries around the world, have attempted to reduce their costs and improve their bottom line. The smart companies are unwilling to let the difficulty of a decision get in the way of what they know is the right thing to do. For instance, they are going to find out who the lowest-cost producer in the world is and target their costs. The other companies may go out of business, or become stagnant.

I have also observed several boards from outside the boardroom and engaged in numerous confidential conversations with members of these boards about the challenges they faced and how they handled them. Here is a simplified version of a board meeting welcoming a newly appointed CEO and highlighting the corporation's future outlook. It includes the following remarks:

"Congratulations, Mr. Smith! You are appointed as the company new CEO.
[...]
With respect to the business priorities, what are the first few steps you will take at the time of recession to turn the company around? (Remember that the company is under loss for the last two quarters.)

Market conditions have already forced our industry to reduce our combined workforce through early retirement. The coming years will be filled with significant unemployment. It will continue to be a challenging future.
[...]
The global economic conditions will put our company's competitive abilities to the test during the **years to come**.

We're in a survival mode.
[...]
We are very glad to have you working with us."

Board's Welcome Letter to a Newly Appointed CEO

While the above remarks sound a bit too dramatic and chaotic, you most likely have read similar messages on the front page of many business newspapers or even in your own boardroom; the truth of the matter is that the global (and also domestic) market is increasingly competitive and will never stop. This is becoming the norm. By the year 2030, more than half of the world's GDP will be generated in emerging markets. Given the state of the economy, and in the face of erratic and persistently slow growth in traditional developed economies, corporate executive teams must tap into these higher growth markets to survive. The worldwide workforce has reached an inflection point; everyone is concerned about the record-high levels of unemployment that continue to plague the world's key economies. Traditional industries are contracting and are under pressure from new global markets. Companies must cope with greatly increased domestic and foreign competition. Emerging markets are becoming key players in the demand for talent. At the same time, consumers are forced to live with little—if any—discretionary money.

According to Gartner-Forbes 2012 Board of Directors:

> This may be the most difficult IT maneuver in business—staying vigilant regarding the costs of the organization and playing defense, while summoning the focus to stay on the offense to invest, *compete* and grow. This year's survey shows 40% of board directors believe that the worst is behind them, and that the economy is on the upswing. This means that organizations must weigh the defensive risks of inaction versus the offensive risks of action. (2.5)

Living in a VUCA World

Maintaining a positive balance sheet or a positive value equation in today's corporations, seems to be a constant challenge quarter after quarter. Bob Johansen suggests that we are now living in a VUCA world:

> Volatile, Uncertain, Challenging, and Ambiguous (VUCA)—that's how the U.S. Army War College describes the current

world for which it must prepare military leaders. This world presents dilemmas not just for the military, but also for us in our businesses. Rapid technological changes, increasing global interconnections, population growth, unstable marketplaces, and income disparities are combining to create a highly volatile and unpredictable terrain. (5.2)

Uncomfortable CEOs must be prepared to respond to low-probability but large-impact events, to accept uncertainty as inevitable and develop strategies for resiliency. The next decade will be far more VUCA than the previous one. The changes arising from the current economic uncertainty are so deep and persistent that many companies and industries will have to redesign their business models. This obviously means that existing systems and IT solutions should be re-evaluated and adapted.

Your winning alternatives will come from the combination of diversity (lots of different components and alternatives), collaboration (the ability to work together), and partnership (working closely with key stakeholders). Conversely, the payoff for getting it right can be great (accelerated time-to-market). The punishment for being wrong can be devastating.

In that context, your CIO should avoid situations where IT system components continue to grow in scope to paramount dimensions—that is, where the risk of a single IT system component could cause the entire platform to crash down. The four critical risks your CIO faces are:

1. **Competitive Risk.** The threat of competitors getting to market faster, gaining market share, or achieving an insurmountable first-mover advantage through the use of information technology.

2. **Portfolio Risk.** The danger that a corporation is spending too much of its scarce IT dollars and resources on basic operational expenses, instead of on truly transformational investments. We have an environment that needs to watch costs closely while IT demonstrates and executes certain strategic investments.

3. **Execution Risk.** The failure to execute IT initiatives effectively or to deliver critical capabilities to the business, on time and on budget.

4. **Service and Security Risk.** The risk that systems won't be available to support and/or service employees and customers as needed, and failure to properly secure the company's critical data assets.

Resilient Leaders

Colin Powell, former U.S. Secretary of State, once said, "Good leaders are made, not born." I propose an interesting amendment to his famous quote "Good *resilient* leaders are made, not born."

Perhaps the right answer to cope with the inevitable VUCA world is to build a new skill for the new generation of resilient leaders. Let's review that and describe key ideas on how to make leaders "resilient" in our business environment.

Resilient leaders have the ability to cope with stress and adversity. They are able to quickly "bounce back" to a previous state of normal functioning after unexpected business failures and crises.

The two most proven approaches to teach and learn resilient leadership are: on-the-job assignments and the executive mentorship program. Both can be implemented separately. However, combining them makes the business results more effective and satisfactory.

1. On-the-job assignments. Putting leaders in progressively more difficult roles and challenges where they have to make tough decisions, and then give them feedback and support. You should give honest feedback to help them improve and confront those leaders who are not performing well enough using the following five tangible traits:

    - Being resilient, using your strength and flexibility to succeed in a VUCA world;

    - Obtaining good outcomes, despite high-risk status;

- Demonstrating constant competence under stress;

- Recovering from a business crisis or failure; and

- Using growth challenges that make future hardships more tolerable.

2. Executive mentorship program. CEOs' interventions should be directed at a powerful mentorship program to improve the quality of the mentor/mentee relationship and provide a safe, non-threatening environment in which the mentee can ask difficult or sensitive questions. The executive mentor should encourage skill development and should offer perspective on how the mentee's skill level fits with the skill needed for future responsibilities.

Case Study: Cultivating IT Leadership

For a couple of years (2010-2011), I chaired an Executive Development Program (EDP) for a non-profit IT organization in America. Our mission was—at that time—to provide personal development and professional growth opportunities for future IT executives. Our program, cultivated IT executive talent via a caring environment for the mentees to gain access to:

- Exposure and interaction with high-level IT executives and business leaders

- A trusted and non-biased relationship with a senior IT mentor

- Guidance on career-related issues that are unique to IT about leadership.

- Deeper understanding on how the CIOs develop their organizations in terms of core IT competencies and performance metrics.

- And ultimately, an opportunity to elevate leadership thru insightful executive coaching.

As the EDP chairman, I had the opportunity to recognize selected junior IT top performers and recommend them for their class graduation with highest honors, based on a three-selection criteria:

1. Highly ambitious IT professionals with top results and top potential (two levels up versus current level). Really top employees with a mixture of business and technology experience who are aspiring to be extraordinary business leaders.

2. Leaders whose core competencies include: change agent, strategic thinker, visionary, results-driven leader, highly passionate, risk taker, people minded.

3. Based on recognition of outstanding performance and leadership within their companies.

In a nutshell, the EDP goal was aimed at getting the most of the IT mentees via a three-way *win* model (win for the participant companies, win for the mentees, and win for the mentors).

You should start building the future resilient leaders of your company. It is a process that takes time, but it is highly rewarding once you see the results. After all, this is you greatest source of competitive advantage and certainly part of your true legacy once your current CEO assignment comes to an end!

You may want to intentionally shift the focus to strengthen talent identification and development. As the CEO, it is your responsibility to:

• Think strategically and make strategic decisions; create growth and competitive advantage; become the master of the business, the organization, and the core competencies.

• Create an environment that fully leverages your organizational talents, builds on the similarities and know-hows, and values and leverages the differences where they can be constructively applied to business problems or solutions.

Your ultimate test as a CEO is not whether you can deliver outstanding business and financial results, but whether you can coach and teach others to be leaders and to build an organization that is just as successful when you are no longer an active player. Lao-Tzu said in the sixth-century BC:

> *The bad leader is he whom the people despise.*
> *The good leader is he whom the people praise.*
> *The great leader is he whom the people say, "We did it ourselves."*

There are five key things that we can keep in mind:

1. We are now living in a VUCA world.

2. It is going to be a rough journey, but you must be ready and resilient.

3. "Good resilient leaders are made, not born." Get on with it. You should also accept risk and take the time needed to whip the executive mentorship program into good shape.

4. Be prepared to respond to low-probability but large-impact events, and to accept uncertainty as inevitable and develop strategies for resiliency. The payoff for getting it right in IT assessment can be great (accelerated time-to-market). The punishment for being wrong can be devastating.

5. Mary Ann Cloyd, from PwC's Center for Board Governance, suggests that, "Instead of looking for risks in any opportunity, we should also be looking for opportunities in every risk." (5.3)

chapter five

CEO LEADERSHIP ACTIONS

5.1 Work with your Leadership team to get people energized to attack problems confronting your business. Make sure certain conditions exist in the organizations:

(a) A mission worth achieving.

(b) Goals that stretch people's abilities.

(c) A realistic expectation that the team can and will succeed.

(d) A team spirit, "All for one, one for all."

(e) A real sense of urgency.

5.2 Work with your leadership team by guiding a powerful mentorship program for the future top-potential resilient leaders.

5.3 As the job assignments are key, ensure that a viable career development program is in place so IT folks don't get trapped (this was a real problem for IT personnel in the past).

5.4 If you decide to redesign your company business model, get your CIO involved from the very beginning. Discuss what the core systems are and which platform solutions should be re-evaluated and adapted accordingly. Develop an action plan to keep this effort on the radar screen.

chapter six

MOVING PAST THE HYPE

*Before you become too entranced with gorgeous gadgets
and mesmerizing video displays,
let me remind you that information is not knowledge,
knowledge is not wisdom, and wisdom is not foresight.
Each grows out of the other, and we need them all.*
~Arthur C. Clarke

Let's start this chapter with some important IT facts. Here are twenty terms that will make you grin, cringe, or run for the nearest dictionary.

Big data	BYOD
Malware	TCP/IP
Web 2.0 (or 3.0 and so on)	Firewalls
Activity Streams	XML
Cloud Computing	Open Source
3D Printing	Conceptual Modeling
Identity Theft	Digital Signatures
Rapid Prototyping	Social Media
SaaS	Near Field Communication
Tablets	Smart Mobs Organizing

While this may be an amusing opening paragraph, it could potentially highlight a very hazardous business behavior. Many IT buzz words have an unclear meaning. If precision is important for your business, using IT buzz words is not the best way to solve your business challenges.

What These IT Buzz Words Mean to Your Business

My simple advice is to avoid IT buzz words altogether. If you happened to engage in an IT buzz word discussion, ask your CIO for a business translation. If you get it, then go with the discussion, if not, stop right there. It would just be a waste of your valuable time.

Polo, my adopted older brother, taught me that there is nothing better than an open and transparent communication to explain complex challenges in simple business terms. Furthermore, he often quotes Albert Einstein's advice that, "If you can't explain it to a six-year-old, you don't understand it yourself."

Understanding Technology Cycles

You may wonder if the IT buzz words you hear in your organization could easily be eliminated with a decree. Would that be a great way to stay focused on your important business priorities? Well, unfortunately, the IT buzz words are most likely here to stay for the long haul. All you need to do is to cope with it more effectively through better understanding.

First of all, using buzz words is common human behavior and a social response to how progress gets embedded in our society. Let's take a historical perspective from the economist Carlota Perez. (6.1) Having researched the circumstances of what happened to the industrial world during the past two and a half centuries, Perez suggests that technological revolutions arrive with remarkable regularity, every half century, and consistently follow an "S" shape, with the following transitions or stages:

1. Beginning of a technological era as *irruption*,

2. The ascent as *frenzy*,

3. The rapid build out as *synergy*, and

4. The completion as *maturity*.

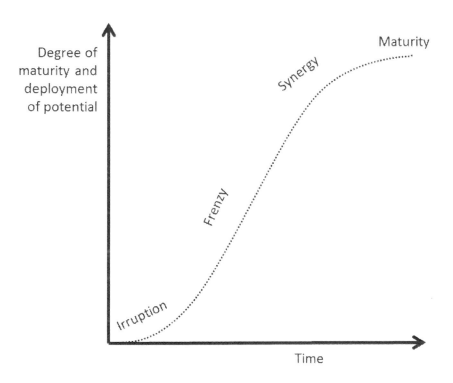

Perez's Trajectory of an Individual Technology (6.1)

Following Perez's model, the macro-technological revolutions can be classified as follows:

- (1771) Industrial Revolution—Britain: Arkwright's mill opens in Cromford

- (1829) Steam and railways—Britain: Test of the "rocket" steam engine for the Liverpool-Manchester railway

- (1875) Steel and heavy engineering—USA: The Carnegie Bessemer steel plant opens in Pittsburgh, Pennsylvania

- (1908) Oil, electricity, the automobile and mass production—USA: First Model-T comes out of the Ford plant in Detroit, Michigan

- (1932) WWI and post-WWII boom—USA: suburban development

- (1971) Information and telecommunications—USA: The Intel microprocessor is announced in Santa Clara, California

- (2015) The hypothetical post-informational technology revolution

Consistent with Perez's research, Gartner similarly defines the IT cycle as following an "S" shape, in this case defined by five rather than Perez's four phases. (6.2) Gartner's helps organizations time the adoption of innovative solutions in the marketplace:

1. "Technological Trigger"—Some technical or conceptual breakthrough that may or may not be associated with a product launch.

2. "Peak of Inflated Expectations"—As publicity increases, so does general excitement with technology. Even if it has seen little or no practical application, there may be some success stories.

3. "Trough of Disillusionment"—As failures mount, interest in the technology begins to wane, and the hype starts to disappear.

4. "Slope of Enlightenment"—A new wave of adoption comes along as the technology matures; proper-use cases are understood more readily.

5. "Plateau of Productivity"—Technological adoption becomes mainstream.

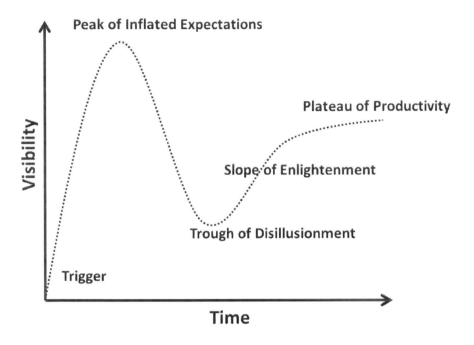

Gartner's Hype Cycle for IT Solutions

In an oversimplified version, this is how the productive society evolves. Our ancestors have applied the "S" shape to deal with technology innovation during the past two and a half centuries and in doing so, they have also used buzz words. Through decades of economic achievement and industrial progress, leaders and inventors have used the "trial and error" model, to find an economically stable platform that maximizes their ideas. Afterwards, a new and—perhaps subtle—revolution comes into play, and the cycle repeats itself.

Once in a while, your CIO may propose to the executive leadership team a totally new IT solution; something so new and entirely disruptive that nobody has ever thought it to be feasible in the company (i.e., think about designing an entirely new airplane [Dreamliner 787] using composite materials for its airframe and claiming to be 20 percent more fuel efficient than its reliable cousin 767). As part of assessment study, I would recommend you to consider a deeper discussion about its benefits and negatives using

Gartner's Hype Cycle for IT Solutions. For perspective, if the strategic plans recommend a best-of-breed approach to win in the marketplace and have a uniquely distinctive differentiation versus your competitors, perhaps a "technological trigger" might be a good alternative.

However, if the plan is to reduce liabilities and risks associated with any innovative market solution, you may want to wait and watch for a while longer and let others test and embrace it before. As a rule of thumb, being an "early adopter" or "trendsetter" gives a higher competitive edge with higher risks and possible incremental costs; while being a "wait and watch" adopter until the solution is broadly accepted and stable increases reliability. In the end, it really depends on your business strategies; _your IT portfolio should always be synchronized to the company's strategic imperatives._

The Hypothetical Post-Informational Technology Revolution

According to Perez's predictions, we are approaching the end of the current age of information and telecommunications. This means that technological adoption becomes mainstream and many corporations should adopt generic information technologies to optimize routine and transactional work, allowing them more time to invest in core competitive advantages. In other words, we will see a significant emphasis and intense effort focused on productivity, adopting new IT capabilities. This is not a commoditization of IT services, but rather a broader and deeper business relevance using IT solutions in practically all of the business core work processes.

Would such a move be bad? Not necessarily. When technology is broadly understood, the benefits begin to outweigh the negatives. I also expect that a significant portion of our IT professionals may shift from having buzz word-driven discussions in their cubicles to leading business conversations about the social and human implications to adopt proven IT solutions in the marketplace.

Interestingly, on the people side, sooner rather than later, your CIO should review and upgrade the IT talent pool with a new set of skills. The new IT professional will be proficient and capable in the following areas:

1. Strong business and people acumen.

2. Robust experience in analyzing data, judgment, and intuition based on experience, and expert knowledge to make informed and timely business decisions.

3. The ability to enable self and others to achieve the vision by leveraging strengths and removing barriers to success.

IT know-how is a minimum requirement, but may not be sufficient to excel and outperform.

A new business "pattern" has begun to emerge as a result of the post-informational technological revolution. The new insight is accurately described by Jim Collins:

> Great companies first build a culture of discipline and create a business model that fits squarely in the intersection of three circles: 1) what they can be the best in the world at, 2) a deep understanding of their economic engine and 3) the core values they hold with deep passion. They then use technology to enhance these pre-existing variables, never to replace them. (5.3)

Business leaders, like yourselves, who quickly understand that the IT capabilities are "accelerators" rather than "fixes to wicked problems," will be on the path to great accomplishments.

The Most Popular IT Buzz Word

Let's close this chapter by addressing one of the most popular IT buzz words of all times: "cloud computing" or simply "the cloud." Is this really a new idea? Will it be a real game changer? Everybody is talking about it. There is a plethora of service providers and solutions around the marketplace, including the big software and services firms such as Amazon, Salesforce, Yahoo, IBM, and Microsoft. But what does that mean to your own business?

Will the cloud transform your business now or later? Is it a totally new approach to solve all business problems? Are all of our internal system dependencies well understood by our IT organization to benefit from the cloud? Let's explore it and debunk the myth that cloud computing is new.

The technological concept behind "cloud computing" has been around for more than fifty years. What is new today are the tools, solutions and methodologies addressing key concerns about decentralization, data integrity, speed and obviously, protecting all the distributed data. However, it is merely the latest buzz word for the evolution of a very successful remote computing service launched at Dartmouth College, USA, in 1964.

The Dartmouth Time-Sharing System was the first large-scale time-sharing system to be successfully implemented using up to 300 simultaneous teleprinters and modems—an impressively large number of users at the same time. Dartmouth College researchers dramatically lowered the cost of providing computing capability, made it possible for individuals and organizations to use a computer without owning one, and promoted the interactive use of computers and the development of new applications.

The exact same idea has morphed since 1964 and has been given to a number of similar buzz words such as: ASP, SaaS, PaaS, TeaaS, BaaS, IDEaaS, etc. (Same shape, but with slightly different flavors.)

In plan business English, "cloud computing" is the use of centralized computing resources that are delivered as a service over a distributed network using your business data and certain remote applications. To get a better idea of what cloud computing is and what it can do for your business, here is good definition, published on October 7, 2009, which can be found at the National Institute of Standards and Technology (NIST):

> Cloud computing is a model for enabling convenient, on-demand network access to a shared pool of configurable computing resources (e.g., networks, servers, storage, applications, and services) that can be rapidly provisioned and released with minimal management effort or service provider interaction. (5.4)

As presented above, the new buzz words refer to technological triggers (i.e., new tools and sophisticated algorithms) that often overstate its usefulness versus what it can do and how to evaluate its success in terms of solving real business problems. Let's remember that simplicity is a great virtue for which we all should strive, even though complexity sells better.

There are four key things that we can keep in mind:

1. Don't let IT buzzwords prevent you and your CIO from defining your business needs clearly. Avoid the hype!

2. The "S" shape is a good maturity indicator and an aid in choosing the best timing to apply IT solutions to your business needs.

3. Start assessing the right IT talent pool that your company might require now and in the near future. Don't let the future catch you and your CIO by surprise. It is much better to plan ahead and anticipate the need.

4. Don't let technology vendors contact your business people directly. Such discussions should be managed by qualified IT professionals. As rude as it sounds, many of the vendors tend to sell their IT products to end users as a panacea using a high-impact pitch replete with buzz words: "*Implement this breakthrough, state-of-the-art, high-speed technology and all your business problems will be solved. Guaranteed!*" Obviously, they will leave too many loose ends in those sales pitches, such as data security and systems integration, as well as the entire IT value realization.

CEO LEADERSHIP ACTIONS

6.1 As is the case with any business leader, being clear, direct, and thoughtful with our words is going to work best when communicating to others—in writing and in speech. Ask your CIO to tell you what he or she means, and he or she will be rewarded with better results.

6.2 When exposed to a new IT alternative, ask your CIO in which "S" shape transition it is and how your company can approach it through a simplified for/against analysis. Then let your CIO decide on the right timing for action.

6.3 Discuss with your CIO and leadership team how often you use IT solutions to _replace_ pre-existing variables (such as saving money or solving wicked work processes) instead of _enhanced_ services (such as newer ways to manufacture and commercialize products in the marketplace). Should this continue to be the norm using your company IT assets?

chapter seven

ENGAGEMENT FOR MANAGING COMPLEXITY

All truths are easy to understand once they are discovered;
the point is to discover them.
~Galileo Galilei

Es hört doch jeder nur, was er versteht.
(Everyone hears only what he understands)
~Johann Wolfgang von Goethe

In this chapter, I will first provide a very brief overview of how "Mastering Complexity" was presented at the 2012 World Economic Forum in Tianjin, China. (7.1) I will then highlight the related business challenges and discuss a cyclic five-step engagement process to assess, plan, and execute information technology solutions that deliver business value in uncertain times. I will close with an approach championed by P&G's Andean vice president, Ed Jardine, (7.2) as an idea on the art of overcoming complexity in the simplest way: minimize the small ideas and focus only on the big priorities.

Difference Between *Complicated* and *Complexity*

Manufacturing hybrid cars, for instance, is a complicated engineering process with specific predictable and repeatable outcomes: hybrid vehicles. On the other hand, if you cannot predict—with acceptable levels of accuracy—what your decision could mean to the company, you are in a complex situation.

As an executive consultant, I focus my expertise on complex business challenges and help my clients find predictable alternatives to improve IT's performance.

Complexity is a Big Word!

As mentioned in Chapter Five (Resilience in an Uncertain Marketplace), our world is volatile, uncertain, ambiguous and very complex. Thus, managing complexity is a growing challenge for most organizations, from the political arena, to nonprofits, to universities, as well as to general business. Complexity translates into a massive explosion of unpredictable offers and demands for any given set of products and services for any industry segment. Each alternative may have the potential to hurt your bottom line if the value it delivers in increased revenues does not surpass its real costs.

Different people may have different interpretations: The view from the sales manager's point of view will be quite different from that of a systems analyst or of the company comptroller. Like the old saying goes, "It all depends." Small changes to a seemingly unrelated element in a complex system may lead to large, unpredictable changes over time. This is known as the "butterfly effect" (i.e., the flapping of a butterfly's wings on the Golden Coast of Peru could affect the weather conditions in the Great Lakes).

Complexity may be better represented using elaborated mathematical models. In fact, there are now highly sophisticated information solutions to analyze massive amounts of raw data, coming in real-time waves such as weather forecasting, air traffic control systems, heart-performance monitoring, shopper-pattern analytics, routing algorithms for package deliveries, stock-trading platforms, and so on. While each solution operates in different environments, they all have common characteristics; they manage <u>complex</u> input data patterns and yield <u>valuable</u> tactical insight outcomes in quasi-real time.

I focus our attention now toward a focal point discussed by Zedillo Ponce's in "Mastering Complexity" at the World Economic Forum in Tianjin, China. He argues that:

> Complexity has been there all along, in every field. Today we have the tools to express, analyze, and represent complexity as never before. In the end, you have to make decisions. Question is, how do you react, even if you have a better tool?

> We should always go back to the basics. We cannot respond
> to a complex system with a complex system of decisions. The
> trick is to try to identify critical barriers and address them.
> You do not want to be a control freak. (7.1)

Ponce cautions you that if an IT system offers a complex decision metric
as the output, such output is not really part of the solution you are looking
for, but most likely part of the problem you are attempting to solve!

A similar situation was experienced when I was working for a Chicago
joint venture a few years ago. On the first company day, we started with
a non-integrated IT platform running everything from payroll, orders,
manufacturing, shipping and billing, and even the email platform (all our
systems were inherited from the two legacy companies and coupled together).
However, the salespeople were selling our goods as an already "integrated"
corporation. Evidently our existing IT capability was five to ten years behind
market expectations, so the board of directors quickly acknowledged the
situation and decided to invest heavily on building new integrated systems
and getting them up to speed. Bottom line, for this mid-size joint venture,
all of a sudden, we simultaneously launched approximately 100 enterprise-
wide solutions. It is important to mention that most of those projects were
fully interdependent and complex in nature. Everybody was facing major
challenges. Our customers and distributors were frustrated with the unmet
business capabilities. Key projects got derailed several times and sadly, the
company was investing large amounts of resources.

Our patient CFO was developing critical concerns as he witnessed that
the enterprise-wide IT projects were taking too long and were spending
more than what the joint venture had originally forecasted. His concerns
were valid and reasonable—98 percent of our projects were classified as
"critically important," and were meant to fix broken critical processes, such
as pricing and promotion management. At some point in time, he called
for an urgent conference meeting with the entire IT leadership team and
instructed us to develop a "real-time," "dynamic" master plan solution. In

plain terms, the CFO wanted to have a wide screen monitor in his office where he could personally supervise, on a daily basis, all the IT software development interdependencies, technical debts, architectural challenges, data discrepancies, project financials, delays, and IT barriers for the entire IT development portfolio!

The IT leadership team was instructed to do it ASAP—and evidently tried hard to please him—and embarked into building the project according to his specifications. As you may imagine, we soon realized that building such a project with all the CFO's requirements would be a rather complex system with highly ineffective outputs; the mock-up prototype proved to be totally unreadable and non-operational (i.e., we could not even pinpoint any of the real barriers we were coping with). Ultimately, we convinced our CFO to terminate the project and instead allow us to manage the portfolio with a plain, conventional monthly status report highlighting barriers and challenges in building the integrated platform to run an integrated business.

Echoing Ponce, the "real-time," "dynamic" IT master plan tracking system turned to be too complex and became part of the problem!

A Cyclic Five-Step Engagement Process

Now let's talk about how to define business solutions to cope with complexity using a cyclic five-step engagement process to assess, plan and execute information technology solutions.

The CIO Eureka!© five-step engagement is designed for collaborative teams to work on highly complex projects that deliver business value. Using this, we have delivered immediate results to enable our clients to win in the marketplace.

Step #1—Assess
Finding the Business Relevance in IT

In this step, I will start the engagement with questioning everything about how to find the business relevance of IT. At the same time, we may be shocked to realize that no matter how sophisticated your IT organization may be, it is still dealing with common traits (or failures?) in some areas the world is facing today. This poses the question: *What is wrong?* Key deliverables in this step include:

- Insights about IT performance and capabilities.

- Guidelines for the balanced success criteria.

Step #2—Envision

Providing Growth Scenarios and Success Measures

A key lesson learned is that we have to embrace complexity and at the same time be selective. Leaders should go back to the basics to make the necessary decisions. During this step, our key deliverables are:

- The key role of the CIO.

- Variability of business growth scenarios.

- Advice to the company planning group.

- Completion of the balanced success criteria.

Step #3—Plan

Building a Plan for Quick Scale and Impact

During this stage, we invest quality time to build the IT solutions using a plan for quick scale and impact. The most efficient and effective method of planning is face-to-face conversation. In this step, the following important deliverables are completed:

- Identify and establish the project team.

- Identify and use business differentiators via rapid prototyping.

- Update the IT master plan.

- See that the scope oversight structure is in place.

Step #4—Enroll

Ensuring Energy and Focus to Keep the IT Portfolio In Line

When you think about the millions of dollars your organization spends each year on IT work programs, wouldn't it be good to know that employees actually understand and more importantly, embrace the reason behind the changes? In this step, we keep the IT portfolio on track as per the balanced success criteria and set the basic expectations so that the sponsors, IT resources, and end users should be able to maintain at a constant pace indefinitely. The key deliverables are:

- Rigor and focus will be reinforced.

- Team norms will be adjusted if performance deviates.

- Change management plan will be defined and validated.

- Execute—ensuring that balanced success criteria are met and/or exceeded.

Step #5—Execute

Ensuring the Balanced Success Criteria are Met and/or Exceeded

In this step, you will see that business and IT people are already building some IT solutions in a collaborative fashion daily and throughout the project. The project team is work as a high-performing team, identifying business requirements and resolving them—perhaps even *before* they arise. The key delivery of success is:

- Market adoption completed as per the value identified in the plan.

This is a very iterative and incremental engagement process design with the purpose of driving successful adoption at the user community. As in any learning environment, the project team reflects on how to become more effective, then tunes and adjusts the five steps accordingly and continues to move on.

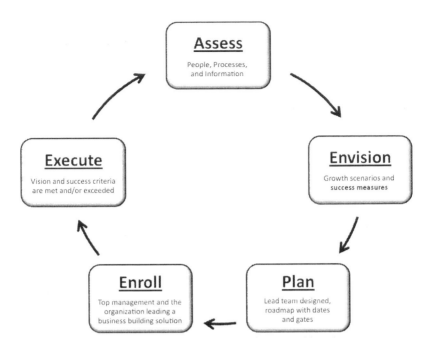

The CIO Eureka!© Five-Step Engagement for Managing Complexity

The Art of Overcoming Complexity

According to Ed Jardine (7.2), "Small ideas equal big problems." The best way to address the most complex challenges is to focus on the simplest idea. Reduce the small ideas and focus only on the big priorities: *No one works on anything else!* This requires identifying the few vital elements with the highest identified value and decisively driving them to success by doing a better job one at a time, and stopping any distraction or investment of resources (people, money, and time) on ideas less relevant to you and your organization.

The Small Ideas Syndrome

Let's illustrate the Small Ideas Syndrome using one of Ed Jardine's case studies. Back in 2000, Venezuela was facing the beginning of a difficult economic situation that affected local consumption. The local P&G marketing organization had insisted to upper management on the need to increase their marketing funds for multiple merchandising activities to increase consumption. After Jardine was appointed vice president for P&G Venezuela and the Andean region (2001), he ran a comparative analysis to determine the real effectiveness of the increased spending behind marketing plans that had been implemented.

	2001	Change vs. year ago
# of Activities	1,701	+800%
Volume (Cases sold)	147,000	+4%
Promotional funds	96,000	+96%

The number of activities had mushroomed by 800 percent, behind a 96 percent increase in spending, while the volume remained stable (+4 percent). What happened was that in response to a difficult business situation, the organization reverted to their comfort zone—it felt right "[to take] a great number of steps to address the declining business trends." This resulted in a plethora of activities.

Unfortunately, the analysis showed that out of these 1,701 initiatives, only 100 made a significant contribution to shareholder value. One hundred out of 1,701! To help the organization understand the problem, he coined the "Small Ideas Syndrome" slogan to enlist the organization's efforts in stopping all of the small activities and to focus instead on the big initiatives (big brands/big customers) with much better potential payouts. This generated significant levels of discomfort in the organization—reducing activity levels during a business downturn was counterintuitive, as well as… "uncomfortable."

Recognizing that this Small Ideas Syndrome was not specific to Venezuela but rather, endemic throughout the company, he also decided to share his case study to help his peers in Latin America. His key takeaways are:

Let's review first what causes people to create small ideas. Your employees may have an inconsistent and fragmented user experience across the enterprise and the consumers they served. They may also have an inability to identify or to work on the right issues. Clearly, this inability turns out to be a failure to focus on the big business priorities as they will find ways to create new opportunities and to fill their agenda with activities. The result will be the perpetuation of a cycle that is difficult to stop by upper management. Perhaps, you should also consider that your people's jobs are too small, so they create additional tasks and projects. And importantly, you and your leadership team may be failing to help the organization make choices, as well as too many priorities.

What is the effect on the people and the business? Evidently you will notice a lack of focus and some significant frustration within the organization. You are probably wasting valuable resources (talent, time, and money) and probably your entire product funding that does not bring incremental value, since it gets diluted into many small ideas. Bottom line, your business results are suboptimal and there is an absence of bold goals and results with small returns; your enterprise is not on a real business transformation.

What can you, the leadership team, do? You should demand a higher quality of execution. Consistently, question and eliminate all activities that do not add real value and are not absolutely critical for achieving strategic goals. In terms of personal development, you should set clear expectations with your people and hold them accountable. And lastly, you should always reward results, rather than activities!

In essence, what are the top five "Small Ideas Syndrome" we must do?

1. We must not spend an extraordinary amount of time and resources focusing on small ideas (i.e., incremental improvements that simply cannot justify what we put into them and do not significantly improve the business).

2. We must identify the true potential of an initiative up front, assess its potential risks, and find out what it takes to grow it.

3. We must work on the root cause of issues rather than testing a lot of magic fixes.

4. We must reward work based on *results*, rather than on the quantity of plans.

5. We must ensure that functional priorities do not overshadow business priorities. Leaders should help organizations by providing them with choices. *What's in/what's out* on projects must be agreed on quarterly business reviews. And remember, **"No one works on anything else!"**

P&G invested resources and ended up with a business distraction that was ultimately turned into an important learning. The Latin American P&G organization became cognizant and channeled all of its energies towards bigger marketing plans. Unfortunately, there is no single answer that applies to every situation like this. You simply have to depend on your judgment, assess the situation and craft the principles to your particular circumstances, and ultimately do what you believe is the right thing. The Small Ideas Syndrome is just one of many approaches to managing complexity, but it is as pragmatic and direct as it can possibly be.

+ + +

There are three key things that we can keep in mind:

1. Mihata states: "The behavior of complex systems is often unpredictable in the straightforward sense that we cannot anticipate the future state of a system, given knowledge of initial conditions…Short-term prediction may be possible—for example, we can easily predict the weather minutes ahead, but not months ahead." (7.3) Your company should view instability and its "challenging implications" as a common characteristic of doing business in the twenty-first century.

2. Complexity causes businesses to change in fundamental ways. Business leaders who are not prepared will never know what hit them. A company seeking uniformity, control from the top, stay-still and rigor with its interrelationships with an environment that is inherently unpredictable, is bound to meet with failure. It will reinforce its strengths and minimize its blind spots, but ultimately will succumb to a dynamic competition. The case study on Borders is very eye opening. The forty-year-old Michigan-based bookseller succumbed to its flexible rival Barnes & Noble (B&N), but Amazon forced both their hands (in terms of online sales and the cost/discounting model—and eventually comprehensiveness). They both responded poorly, but Borders made out worse than B&N. And arguably, B&N has weathered the storm better for reasons beyond Internet sales. That is, B&N has been flexible, but not just in terms of Internet commerce. Things such as its self-published public domain titles, private labels, etc., have given them bigger cuts of sales, for example.

3. Forward-thinking leaders understand that a winning company should aim to position itself in a region of discomfort. Discomfort does not necessarily form character, but it certainly reveals it. Try to steer your organization toward the edge of discomfort; dive into it and then come back with the vision, direction, and decisions needed.

CEO Leadership Actions

chapter seven

7.1 Are you getting the real story from the front lines of your business? **Does your company** have the ability to analyze and represent complexity? Your CIO could give insights into the relationships between people in the company and how information flows really **happen.**

7.2 Discuss the "Small Ideas Syndrome" with your executive leadership team and decide how to deploy it in your organization.

7.3 Ask your CIO to share the company's engagement methodology with the executive leadership team and explore improvement areas. Try this with fewer ideas and projects.

chapter eight

A Culture of IT Innovation

Innovation is the specific instrument of entrepreneurship.
The act that endows resources with
a new capacity to create wealth.
~Peter F. Drucker

In a recent interview with McKinsey, the U.S. chief technology officer, Todd Park said, "Today, innovation is almost always supported—if not driven—by technology." (8.1) This may be true in the way we live, study and even work. However, there is an interesting irony about IT organizations: Most IT executives prefer NOT to innovate. Why? It's too risky! The IT executives quite often default to a corporate culture about controls, structure, rigor, and planning.

In this chapter, I will discuss that while controls, rigor, and planning are key in any corporation, it is also important to embrace a culture of IT innovation. Changing the nature of IT work is key to moving away from a "No, this will not work," to a "Yes, let's look at the relevant value these ideas may bring to the business and from there, we will decide next moves" culture. In other words, moving your IT organization from maintenance to innovation will drive commensurable incremental value. Instead of the typical ethos that has characterized most IT organizations, you should bring a powerful sense of openness, transparency and empowerment. I will also present a practical framework to guide your innovation engagement rules.

Five Indispensable Elements for Business Innovation

Innovation was derived from the Latin word, *innovaree,* meaning "to make something new," although understanding its full concept remains difficult. The five **indispensable** characteristics that define business innovation are:

- **Wealth:** Must create perceived benefits (i.e., shareholders' value).

- **Risk:** It is just like "walking off the cliff blindfolded." However, the higher the risk, the greater the reward.

- **Sustainability:** Time to grow up, develop and evolve into something valuable.

- **Diversity:** A combination of diverse ideas placed into new domains.

- **Selection:** The best will win. Even slight advantages are important when selected.

Innovation has been a long (intense, albeit exciting) journey for many corporations. Like many of you, they have learned that innovation is not just an event or a new item. It is not just a process or a portfolio of patents. Perhaps that is what we thought it was several years ago. But is innovation merely a mechanical process or is it actually a complex adaptive system? In 1998, Peter F. Drucker said that "new opportunities rarely fit the way an industry has always approached the market, defined it, or organized to serve it." (8.2) In an analogy to Mother Nature, it is the combined outcome of adaptive capabilities (diversity, selection, risk and sustained reapplication).

Can you imagine a company that prides itself on its innovative capabilities being successful only half of the time and for only part of its categories or product lines? Winning companies that succeed year after year have learned two magic secrets about innovation:

1. It is a mandatory requirement for sustained growth.

2. It has to occur across the enterprise. Everywhere. It's up to the

leaders to foster an environment where all employees get involved with some kind of innovation. Ensuring that all contributing, all collaborating, and all valued elements are present helps to ensure that the best ideas rise to the top and are acted upon. Perhaps most importantly, it has been learned that the best innovation ideas seldom come from the top. This is all the more reason why a diverse organization is so vitally important.

Jack Welch, the former CEO of GE and a living embodiment of business innovation, argues that "although people often think innovation is limited to practical scientific advances, it's much more than that. It's about business expansion." He goes even further, stating that, "To innovate something is as important as inventing it."

Innovation is not important only to the company. Innovation is also important to IT professionals. To innovate, IT must become a driver of strategic change. **<u>Do not expect any less!</u>**

Innovation is the life blood of any business in the twenty-first century. It is critically important that companies bring innovation to their clients. Innovation not only drives many consumption/usage metrics, it also helps you to identify and adapt to new changes in modern society, such as: a) the evolution of visualization capabilities with increasing infographics, or; b) the shifting of power to the consumers, which now requires companies to meet new and exacting consumer demands and facilitate real and differentiated consumer experiences.

In essence, innovation drives a collaborative and creative process for a win/win negotiation. Channawi defines this very clearly:

> In a win/win negotiation, your task is to "create" as much value as possible for you and for the other side. Often, the two sides' interests do not compete at all. Their task is to arrive at a deal that integrates their interests as efficiently as possible. Cooperation carries no cost here; indeed, cooperation and

disclosure of information make you even more effective. In a win/win negotiation, there are often many items or issues to be negotiated; opportunities for creativity abound and the relationship between the two negotiators is often highly valued. (8.3)

Ideas and tools are critical elements for innovation to create concept and patents. However, the number of great concepts is irrelevant if it is gathering dust on your shelves. Real value is created only when those great concepts become reality in the marketplace and the target users use them consistently. The final goal for innovation is and always will be to create wealth, not just to create ideas and concepts.

From a business standpoint, the IT opportunities are clear. Information technology will:

- Deliver faster and better innovation (intentional and agile) that can be scaled in a sustainable way.

- Improve business propositions with strong financial business cases.

- Improve the IT alignment process with the key stakeholders (i.e., beneficiaries, implementers, payers).

- Bring a step-change speed of transition from project incubation (prototyping) through initiatives and market adoption.

A Funnel for IT Innovation

By establishing a deliberated process to manage IT innovation you will be able to reshape how your company finds, identifies and then translates ideas into successful prototypes resulting in efficient hand offs to previously identified project initiatives, or future new project evaluations.

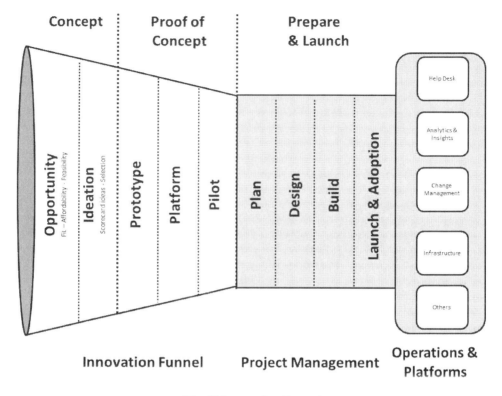

The IT Innovation Funnel

According to Gupta, (8.4) the notion of the funnel is widely popular in the innovation industry. Lots of ideas enter the funnel, very few exit as new solutions, and the rest are weeded out. A funnel raises the bar, strengthens the discipline, and ultimately hands off the prototype to the program management organization to bring solutions into the marketplace.

While everybody needs to be part of the innovation culture, a small team in your IT organization needs to be accountable to assist you with the innovation capability. Let's call it the "innovation funnel team," or IFT for short. Your IFT should be as diverse as possible, and should work with the company strategy team by identifying ideas that substantially improve your ability to compete. IFT provides a venue to test riskier ideas in a controlled environment and break down silos across multiple company teams. Once the new idea turns into a workable solution or prototype, IFT will also eliminate barriers to adoption/change and deliver priorities efficiently. The funnel systematically converts ideas into projects.

However, very little attention has been paid to how to initially submit new good ideas to the IFT. Should your company welcome hundreds of ideas into the funnel? Your employees may have plenty of ideas for new information technology solutions, but the true innovation is about reducing the risk while focusing on ideas with the highest credible shareholder return. Let us now discuss how to help people get ideas defined, qualified (i.e., selection criteria), and guided to explore fertile ideas on innovation.

I have seen three types of ideas that people often submit for IT innovation:

- Ideas that would require a very significant up front investment.

- Ideas that would simply be irrelevant for the core business in which we operate.

- Ideas that are too futuristic, for which the necessary technology does not yet exist or which we simply cannot afford to acquire.

Although interesting and thought-provoking, evaluating those ideas would be unsuitable and result in a waste of time and resources.

At the same time, ignoring those ideas will most likely demoralize the employees who submitted them. It is essential for management to communicate the selection criteria very clearly. Each employee needs to know and appreciate the relevance of the selection criteria (which I will define shortly). This transparency will strengthen an environment structured to understand the innovation framework and the rationale for the IFT to select and deselect ideas. If this is not communicated clearly, your employees will think that the selection process is not truly inclusive and may opt out from the culture of innovation. Good leadership will see that all functions and business teams have enough leeway to submit new IT ideas and follow a united process for selection.

I designed an easy-to-use innovation engagement model with three elements to preselect ideas:

- **Fit**: Does the initiative fit in with the company strategy?

- **Affordability**: Does the IFT believe that the initial ROI (return on investment) is relevant enough for the company to dedicate team time and resources to the initiative?

- **Feasibility**: Does the IFT believe it is feasible to complete this request with existing resources and adequate external IT partnerships?

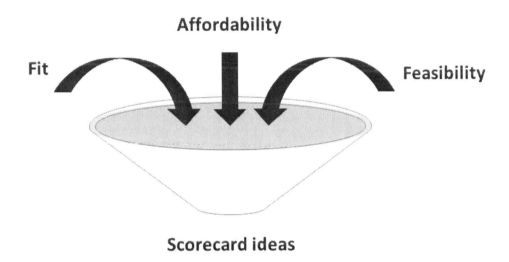

The FAF (Fit-Affordability-Feasibility) Selection Criteria

The FAF (Fit-Affordability-Feasibility) elements are part of the scorecard selection criteria. The FAF scorecard accelerates the discussion among the IFT and quickly moves concepts toward a prototype-stage gate, where the targeted end user will sense how the solution may work well before we proceed with the establishment of a formal project.

Once an idea has passed the initial FAF selection criteria, it flows through the funnel and successfully reaches a point of decision, which could be any of the following:

1. Idea success is sufficient to launch into the company IT portfolio without further escalation or financial commitment.

2. Prototype can be taken to the IT baseline cost structure (i.e., some training or rollout may be required).

3. Prototype is successful, but must be scaled for a company decision as the prototype is large enough and should be handed off to the projects team for future portfolio inclusion. The IFT will deliver a proof of concept documentation with the preliminary business case and details to move project in to the planning phase of the company's project methodology.

4. Prototype shows insufficient value to continue. This idea is eliminated with no further work.

The funnel and the FAF selection criteria will ensure a more robust and constant stream of new ideas. They will offer practical ways to prototype versions before they are turned into formal project initiatives.

Organizing for Innovation

How do you create an IT organizational culture that encourages risk-taking, creativity and continuous adaptation required for innovation? Uncomfortable CEOs are quick to talk about "celebrating failure" (8.5)—instead of lowering your information technology failure rate, simply lower the cost of failure, learn faster and apply the lessons to your business. The FAF focuses the discussion on improvements and creates a well-connected culture of IT innovation.

Innovation is not a hobby; it needs to be sustainable, scalable and focused on results, just like any other function in the company. Organizations designed for innovation have three defining characteristics:

- New ideas permeate throughout the company freely and quickly.

- The companies are flexible and receptive to learning from success and failure and managing ambiguity.

- They transform ideas into proven concepts consistently and profitably.

A company organized around those characteristics will bring differentiated solutions to the market, more quickly, less expensively and more creatively. In others words, innovation creates wealth (i.e., shareholder value).

As described in Moisés Noreña's white paper, *Whirlpool Innovation Journey*:

> One of the essential business skills for leaders as well as innovation architects is having an ability to read the times and knowing what will work for the particular state of the organization, the internal and external environments, as well as the leadership in place. (8.6)

An organization must build teams that are diverse in talent, and fit individuals into the right roles to drive success. In *The Nature of Innovation*, P. Zablock shares a perspective about the common people characteristics across innovation:

> **Innovators** are players who introduce something new. They search for new ideas, successes and failures, both big and small. They are your idea incubators and feeders. In order to be successful, it is important for them to have a convenient mechanism with which to pass on their ideas to the gatekeepers and change agents.
>
> **Gatekeepers** are critical to success because they understand how resources are managed in the company and understand who has the authority to supply them with people, money

and systems. They also provide rigor and discipline following agreed-to control stages. They would be your primary selection to staff the "Innovation Funnel Team" mentioned earlier. They tend to understand what will benefit the organization and are normally in management positions.

Change Agents. Their role is to drive adoption—the diffusion of solutions and services. They are able to explain and effectively communicate the difference between change and transitions. They will play a pivotal role in managing of resistance to change, especially during periods of decline or retrenchment in organizations. This is a very difficult role, often ignored and/or neglected. The change agents have a unique ability to speak different languages with different communities: they can speak the language of creativity with the innovators; the language of structure and processes with information technology leaders; and more importantly, the language of business with managers. (8.7)

Organizing is just the first move. You need to enable the entire team to go beyond accepted ideas, to generate ways to get better results. Once your team is working at peak performance, they will formalize a repeatable process of innovation using proven ideas and methods. It's amazingly powerful when you get your people developing outstandingly clever solutions for new business opportunities.

As mentioned in Chapter Two (Today's Paradigm Shifts to Assess IT Priorities), the "third flow mandate" depends on the ability to jointly innovate with business partners to commercialize that value. This concept becomes even more powerful when your team builds effective networks both internally and externally for learning, sharing and innovation.

When you put all of this together—an organization designed to innovate, and catalytic events that spark even more ideas—you get what is called a culture of IT innovation:

- Big, predictable, profitable innovation equals:

    ~Good ideas, linked to company goals, flowing friction-free across the company.

    ~Times the multiplier of external connections with the best IT solution providers.

    ~Divided by Fit–Affordability–Feasibility selection criteria.

    ~Elevated to seed funding so good ideas get oxygen fast.

There are four key things that we can keep in mind:

1. Fostering diversity to manage innovation is perhaps the best cultural routine your company can establish. This talks about the diversity in the widest possible sense—gender, contributions, strengths, creed, age, style, and thought. Yes, your company may be diverse, but not diverse enough. Most likely you are not yet where you need to be if you want to achieve long-term success (continuous growth and sustained greatness). You need to be ever more diverse.

2. You might consider established innovation and the reapplication of innovation as a key element in your employee performance appraisals. For instance, you might introduce a new core competency (INNOVATION): "1) Approaches opportunities for innovation holistically; considers the total realm of what is available including internal reapplication, external benchmarking and new invention; or, 2) goes beyond accepted ideas, finds new improvement opportunities, generates ways to get better results." (7.7)

3. Since the biggest enemy of innovation is fear—fear of failing on the project deliverables, fear of being singled out, fear of damaging performance appraisals—you should provide assurance that failure is okay as long as there is learning involved. Establishing innovation as an expectation throughout the entire company is crucial; train people on how to innovate and you will celebrate the very best examples of innovation that deliver total shareholder return.

4. Siloed performance objectives is a huge practical problem. Expect to (and do) reward people for cross-fertilization—reapplying the innovation across projects, markets and functions. J. A. Barker defines this as "Innovation at the Verge: as the combining of two or more different elements to create a new territory." (7.8) Organizations that embrace innovation as a strategic growth plank cannot afford to be hung up with a "not-invented-here" mindset.

chapter eight

CEO LEADERSHIP ACTIONS

8.1   Discuss with your CIO about establishing an IFT (innovation funnel team)—the respective pros and cons, and how to keep the IFT from becoming a bureaucratic structure.

8.2   Decide with your CIO how much seeding money is required to start with. It may be good to start small and test the framework before you pursue heavy investments and longer prototyping game-changing ideas.

8.3   A key component for success is broad executive communication. What would be the best way to maintain the company executive team in the loop so that duplicated efforts are minimized (or even eliminated entirely) when it comes to building new IT solutions?

chapter nine

PREPARED TO WIN—BRINGING IT ALL TOGETHER

*The dissemination of business best practices means survival today
and requires speed and innovation
—and greater adoption of information technologies.*
~Paul A. Strassmann
(Executive Advisor, NASA and the Department of Defense)

As discussed, many enterprises have managed IT by focusing on expenses and projects. There is a lot of pressure on executives, and on CIOs in particular, to perform accordingly during this time of economic recovery. The traditional focus has been on reducing people and maintaining a fixed amount of capital investments. IT is deployed at a tactical level to support operations, and the CIO oversees a short-term annual budget that includes most of the company's information technology resources.

What is missing is a good articulation about the business value-in-use of IT.

In this context, the real key question is how the CIO should guide the CEO and the board's awareness beyond the traditional "IT risks and oversight" into a more fulfilling and relevant "IT contribution," and its impact, freeing up capacity for innovation, improving efficiency, managing complexity, and reducing costs. Think about it, and ask yourself, "How does your C-suite think differently about IT?" rather than, "What is the role of IT in building great companies?" (9.2)

The only reason to make an IT investment is to realize business value. Linking that business value to the IT investment requires that the IT applications be totally linked to your company goals. This represents an effort driven by the needs of your consumers, shoppers and customers. It does not represent an effort driven by the need to be digital. The technology pipeline should always be secondary to the emphasis on providing business value.

As discussed throughout this book, the resilient CIOs are not technocrats. They know the science of IT and may also have the necessary business acumen, commercial ability and people management expertise to add considerable strategic value to the business and its shareholders. What they are still lacking is the opportunity to promote their skills and demonstrate both the current contribution brought to the business, as well as to enable executives and the boardroom to be aware of what information technology can offer in the future. (9.1)

Here is an excellent quote from the CEO of a Top Fortune 500 company when she was interviewed about her thoughts on her CIO. This is what she said to the news reporter:

> My Company's CIO is a strategist. He has a desire to lead from the front and lead by example how we should run the business—and to always play to win, never to lose. There's no winning in business without the right strategies in place; they [IT] have created a model for coming up with the best strategies we can afford, and it's proven to be very effective. IT never starts with technologies; they always look at trends in the world that are or may be having an impact on the future of our business.

This is an excellent testimonial about a resilient CIO! Let's aim to go beyond an interesting anecdote and evolve this quote into the norm about describing what is the role of any resilient CIO and even more profoundly, about emphasizing the critical role IT should play in increasing the value in their corporations. There are no insurmountable barriers that prevent any resilient CIO from following such an example.

Success depends heavily on the communication of which IT service levels are needed for each business. By refining and enhancing them, the organization will be able to meet its goals and objectives.

We should not think only about computers, software, and networks as assets; we need to think about other areas to fully realize their full business benefit. Return on information—is the new ROI of the post-information revolution era.

Return on information assets is an area that deserves management attention. Information is the real asset for which you should seek a return.

Indeed, quite a few leading corporations have already defined a novel IT "identity model," to accurately communicate to their employees how IT is about to bring value to the business. For perspective, they have even changed the IT functional name into something more "meaningful" such as "ISI" (information solutions and insights). According to their definition, the unique asset in an "ISI" corporate environment is *information*, while their deliverables to the business are *solutions*, which in turn provide the entire corporation with enhanced and accurate business *insight*. These thought leaders have signaled that, while information remains the function's key asset, its reach goes far beyond mere technology. The focus is more and more on helping in the overall decisions space by enabling more effective business solutions. This should drive a more advanced—and perhaps more effective—approach toward managing business information as one of the company's core assets.

This is a very exciting time as IT faces the opportunities that these changes create for all IT professionals!

A Final Remark about You, the Uncomfortable CEOs

I will be very blunt: CEOs and business leaders are not particularly well-equipped to deliver a strategic IT approach. As a CEO and leader, you are too focused on operational and strategic topics, such as managing cost drivers, engaging with NGOs and consumers, finding new products, and launching new revenue sources. If you think you are equipped to deliver such an approach, this implies that you should really understand the implications of new, rapidly changing and complex IT systems and processes for the current business model, or perceive a strategic potential and value in adopting new IT solutions. Are you expecting too much from your own key business deliverables as a CEO?

Allow me to propose a much better alternative. Delegate that responsibility to a resilient CIO.

You should think carefully about the right skill set for the right candidate. Hiring and nurturing a CIO who focuses on technology without the context of business processes, business productivity, and business value is a "bad" management decision. A resilient CIO is a leader who knows how to build the bridge between IT and business goals. The resilient CIO is also a leader who explicitly addresses information as an enterprise asset, and understands what is on your agenda and how IT fits into it. More than other senior executives, your resilient CIO should have the capability to build trust, communicate and collaborate with others with exceptional levels of diplomacy and discretion. Ultimately, he or she is a leader who creates and shapes an IT organization to leverage efficiency, effectiveness, and change management with a solid link to the strategic business objectives. Of all the functional C-level roles in your organization, the CIO may hold the most cards; he or she is intrinsically linked to the levers for business strategy, operations, financial realities, and innovation. Without IT, no business would operate and through analytics, your CIO has the greatest impact on productivity and profitability.

Think carefully about who should be your resilient CIO and which role expectations are needed to make your company an even greater one.

Will there be changes? There might be. A great driver of human evolution has been the increase in connectivity for the exchange ideas. I don't expect everyone to take what I wrote as if it were written in stone.

However, I do expect that all of my CEO readers will be committed to the goal of working hard and helping every IT professional be accountable in generating business value using the five IT leadership success criteria described in Chapter Four (Success Criteria Lead to Success): partnership, strategic focus, velocity, frugality, and execution. It pays!

There are four key things that we can keep in mind:

1. **Be resilient.** The real importance of resilience is to separate emotions from the decision-making process. The first thing that is very important is not to panic and to think through decisions and to plan. You need to make wise financial decisions and the correct decisions for your own company.

2. **Treat time as a precious commodity.** Get on with it. You should also accept risk and take the time needed to get the information needed to make a good decision. But once you have made it, resist overintellectualized and overcomplicated decisions. Concentrate your decisions on the substance, not the form of issues.

3. **Research opportunities.** Continue to research other potential opportunities that may be out there. It's important to constantly look and understand other opportunities. For example, Alvin Toffler said, "The illiterates of the 21st century will not be those who cannot read and write, but those who cannot learn, relearn, and unlearn."

4. **Identify practical values.** The misconception is that because the economy is bad there are no opportunities out there. For example, the acceleration of innovation to market. Consumers and users want one-on-one connections to any service or product they interact with, so you have to respond with new IT solutions. This is thoroughly changing the way you operate—the always-on, instant nature of interaction today.

CEO Leadership Actions

chapter nine

9.1 Engage in a one-to-one working relationship to build your CIO's confidence. This sends a message that the CEO truly sees the role as strategically important.

9.2 Keep favoring your CIO's drive to design the way your company conducts its business.

9.3 You should ask your CIO to drive innovation through sound and compelling plans that will ultimately benefit your corporation.

CEO Leadership Actions

Throughout this book, I have explored progressive ideas related to finding the business value of information technology and importantly enhancing your time with your CIO and key IT associates.

Mahatma Gandhi famously encouraged everyone to "be the change you wish to see in the world." *The Uncomfortable CEO*™ reading experience should guide your steps to lead your IT organization into the highest-leveraged function. The following thirty *CEO Leadership Actions* were written to make the most of the competitive advantage between the CEO and the IT community at large. By honestly following them all, you will strengthen your company's ability to be fast, flexible, responsive and versatile in the rapidly changing business environment of this twenty-first century. Remember nothing important ever happens when you are comfortable.

The following are the *CEO Leadership Actions*. Create a checklist to review key ideas and more importantly, agree with your CIO about a radically different approach to transform your IT organization quickly and effectively. Use this list as a guide to define the future vision of the business and information technology in your own business—let's say in a three- to five-year horizon.

CEO Leadership Actions

chapter one
Who Are The Uncomfortable CEOs?

1.1   Think briefly about yourself and other leaders in your leadership team and consider how well you reflect the virtues of an uncomfortable CEO.

1.2   Discuss your findings with your leadership team. Create a list of expectations to shape the new virtues.

chapter two
Today's Paradigm Shifts to Assess IT Priorities

2.1   Increase and improve quality time with your CIO. Try to understand first. Your CIO will be initially pleased with the opportunity to talk to you about his or her functional responsibilities.

2.2   Discuss with your board organizational commitments to changing the role of the CIO and define CIO objectives to encourage operating "radically differently."

2.3   Discuss with your CIO plans for the board to become digitally literate and help them to understand how IT is paramount in gaining competitive advantage.

2.4   Discuss with your CIO plans for the board to become digitally literate, and help them to understand how IT is paramount in gaining competitive advantage.

2.5   Explore ideas with your CIO to change the conversation from "IT risk" to "IT contribution." What needs to be done?

chapter three
Reflections on Value

3.1   Analyze your current IT game plan (IT portfolio) in terms of the four key value drivers. Assign priorities based on the "best" value promised.

3.2   Explore one or two value-in-use metrics with your CIO. Is the value rendered worth the effort? What can you *stop, start, and continue*?

3.3   How effectively is your company driving a culture of IT value-creation? Qualify strengths and opportunities with the OP Model hexagon.

chapter four
Success Criteria Lead to Success

4.1   Compare your existing project success criteria with the proposed "balanced" success criteria for IT projects. Make the necessary adjustments.

4.2   Privately coach your CIO on the variability of growth scenarios. If you need for IT to be more flexible, your company must be in a position to do better "what-if" planning.

4.3   Ask your CIO about the current IT identity model. It may be time to rethink the way IT operates; your CIO should come up with a new identity model. Suggest ideas to "put money to work." And publicly commend IT with the examples you appreciate.

4.4   Adjust your CIO and IT leadership team performance appraisals using the five-element IT equity organization success criteria.

chapter five
Resilience in an Uncertain Marketplace

5.1   Work with your leadership team to get people energized to attack problems confronting your business. Make sure certain conditions exist in the organizations:

(a) A mission worth achieving.

(b) Goals that stretch people's abilities.

(c) A realistic expectation that the team can/will succeed.

(d) A team spirit, "All for one, one for all."

(e) A real sense of urgency.

5.2   Work with your leadership team by guiding a powerful mentorship program for the future top-potential resilient leaders.

5.3   As the job assignments are key, ensure that a viable career development program is in place so IT folks don't get trapped (this was a real problem for IT personnel in the past).

5.4   If you decide to redesign your company business model, get your CIO involved from the very beginning. Discuss what the core systems are and which platform solutions should be re-evaluated and adapted accordingly. Develop an action plan to keep this effort on the radar screen.

chapter six
Moving Past the Hype

6.1   As is the case with any business leader, being clear, direct, and thoughtful with our words is going to work best when communicating to others—in writing and in speech. Ask your CIO to tell you what he or she means, and he or she will be rewarded with better results.

6.2   When exposed to a new IT alternative, ask your CIO in which "S" shape transition it is and how your company can approach it through a simplified for/against analysis. Then let your CIO decide on the right timing for action.

6.3   Discuss with your CIO and leadership team how often you use IT solutions to _replace_ pre-existing variables (such as saving money or solving wicked work processes) instead of _enhanced_ services (such as newer ways to manufacture and commercialize products in the marketplace). Should this continue to be the norm using your company IT assets?

chapter seven
Engagement for Managing Complexity

7.1   Are you getting the real story from the front lines of your business? **Does your company** have the ability to analyze and represent complexity? Your CIO could give insights into the relationships between people in the company and how information flows really **happen.**

7.2   Discuss the "Small Ideas Syndrome" with your executive leadership team and decide how to deploy it in your organization.

7.3   Ask your CIO to share the company's engagement methodology with the executive leadership team and explore improvement areas. Try this with fewer ideas and projects.

chapter eight
A Culture of IT Innovation

8.1   Discuss with your CIO about establishing an IFT (innovation funnel team)—the respective pros and cons, and how to keep the IFT from becoming a bureaucratic structure.

8.2   Decide with your CIO how much seeding money is required to start with. It may be good to start small and test the framework before you pursue heavy investments and longer prototyping game-changing ideas.

8.3   A key component for success is broad executive communication. What would be the best way to maintain the company executive team in the loop so that duplicated efforts are minimized (or even eliminated entirely) when it comes to building new IT solutions?

chapter nine
Prepared to Win—Bringing It All Together

9.1   Engage in a one-to-one working relationship to build your CIO's confidence. This sends a message that the CEO truly sees the role as strategically important

9.2   Keep favoring your CIO's drive to design the way your company conducts its business.

9.3   You should ask your CIO to drive innovation through sound and compelling plans that will ultimately benefit your corporation.

If you successfully and honestly complete the above thirty CEO leadership actions, we are now at a crossroads; your traditional view of the IT function has been revisited. I am confident that the worst is behind you and you will now be on the upswing.

Index

NOTES

(1.1) Pepper, J. E. (1999) *Does Character Count*, The Procter & Gamble Company Chairman of the Board lecture at Miami University—March 15, 1999.

(2.1) Kuhn, T. (1962) *The Structure of Scientific Revolutions*, University of Chicago. He crafted the notion of "paradigm shifts" as the profound change that takes place in the basic assumptions when the society adopts a new model to interpret reality.

(2.2) Cohn, J. & Robson, M. (2010) *Taming Information Technology Risk*, Oliver Wyman, NACD, www.nacdonline.org/files/Taming%20Information%20Technology%20Risk%20Final.pdf.

(2.3) Bloch, M. & Blumberg, S. (2012) *Delivering Large-Scale IT Projects, On Time, On Budget and On Value*, McKinsey & Company.

(2.4) Hunter, R. & Westerman, G. (2009) *The Real Business of IT*, Harvard Business Press.

(2.5) Raskino, M. & Lopez, J. (2012) Gartner-Forbes 2012 Board of Directors Survey: *Stay in Balance*, Gartner Research G00234126 http://my.gartner.com/portal/server.pt?open=512&objID=202&&PageID=5553&mode=2&in_hi_userid=2&cached=true&resId=2066115&ref=AnalystProfile.

(2.6) Internet World Stats (Dec 2011) *Internet Usage Statistics—The Big Picture*, www.internetworldstats.com/stats.htm.

(2.7) Google stats (2008) Google Stats, www.google.com.

(2.8) James, J. (June 2012) *How Much Data is Created Every Minute?*, www.domo.com/blog/2012/06/how-much-data-is-created-every-minute/.

(2.9) Carr, N. G. (May 2003) *IT Doesn't Matter*, Harvard Business Review.

(2.10) King, J. (April 24, 2012) *CIO.IN Magazine*, http://www.cio.in/news/thirty-five-percent-enterprise-it-expenditures-outside-corporate-it-budget-ga

(2.11) Scott, R. D. (2011) *Identifying and Building Core Competencies: Discovering Your Strengths & Executive Leadership*, HITEC mentorship webinar.

(2.12) Needles, C. (2012) *Troubling Gaps Between IT and Business Executives, Hamper Innovation and Business Growth*, CA Technologies.

(2.13) Prensky, M. (2001) *Digital Natives, Digital Immigrants, On the Horizon*, MCB University Press, Vol. 9 No. 5.

(3.1) Walters, D. (2002) *Operations Strategy*, Palgrave Macmillan.

(3.2) P&G (Sept 2005) *Global Business Services*, The Procter & Gamble Company internal memorandum.

(3.3) Hanna, D. P. (1988) *Designing Organizations for High Performance*, Addison Wesley.

(4.1) Atkinson, R. (1999) *Project Management: Cost, Time and Quality, Two Best Guesses and a Phenomenon, It's Time to Accept Other Success Criteria*, Department of Information Systems, Business School, Bournemouth University, Dorset BH12 5BB, UK.

(4.2) Farahat, T. (2003) *More with Less*, The Procter & Gamble Company internal memorandum.

(4.3) Meyer, C. (May 1994) *How the Right Measures Help Teams Excel*, Harvard Business Review.

(4.4) Turner, J. R. (1996) Editorial, International Project Management Association, International Journal of Project Management.

(5.1) Pearl, M. (2012) *Grow Globally: Opportunities for Your Middle-Market Company Around the World*, Wiley.

(5.2) Johansen, R. (2012) *Leaders Make the Future*, Berrett Koehler Publishers.

(5.3) Cloyd, M. A. (2012) *Making Sense of IT Risk*, NACD Directorship November/December 2012.

(5.4) Mell, P. (2011) *The NIST Definition of Cloud Computing*, NIST US Department of Commerce/ September 2011.

(6.1) Perez, C. (Sept 2002) *Technological Revolutions and Financial Capital*, Cheltenham, UK.

(6.2) Fenn, J. (June 2008) *Understanding Gartner's Hype Cycles*, www.gartner.com/technology/ research/methodologies/hype-cycle.jsp.

(7.1) Zedillo Ponce, E. (Sept 2012) *Mastering Complexity*, Annual Meeting of the New Champions— World Economic Forum, Tianjin, China.

(7.2) Jardine, E. D. (Nov 2001) *The Small Ideas Syndrome*, The Procter & Gamble Company internal memorandum.

(7.3) Mihata, K. (1997) *The Persistence of Emergence, Chaos, Complexity, and Sociology: Myths, Models, and Theories*, Thousand Oaks.

(8.1) Park, T. (June 2012) *Unleashing Government's "Innovation Mojo,"* Mckinsey Quarterly Report, www.mckinsey.com/insights/public_sector/unleashing_governments_innovation_mojo_an_ interview_with_the_us_chief_technology_officer.

(8.2) Drucker, P. F. (1998) *The Discipline of Innovation*, Harvard Business Press, Reprint 98604.

(8.3) Channawi, O. (2005) *The Art of Negotiation*, The Procter & Gamble Company internal memorandum.

(8.4) Gupta, P. (2011) *The Innovation Solution*, Accelper Consulting/CreateSpace, an Amazon Company.

(8.5) Good, A. (Dec 2012) *The Fail Report 2011*, Engineers Without Borders Canada.

(8.6) Noreña, M. (Jan 2013) *Whirlpool's Innovation Journey: An On-Going Quest for a Rock-Solid and Inescapable Innovation Capability*, Whirlpool Co.

(8.7) Zablock, P. (July 2000) *The Nature of Innovation*, Institute For The Future (ITFT)

(9.1) Lamm, J. (Oct 2011) *The Future Role of the CIO—"Becoming the Boss,"* CA Technologies— CS1782_1011.

(9.2) Collins, J. (Aug 2002) *How Great Companies Tame Technology*, Newsweek Magazine.

About CIO Eureka! LLC

Finding business relevance in IT. Our expertise.

Trusted advisor to CEOs and executives on how to find business relevance in IT. Led by international IT executives from Fortune 30 companies. We work with our clients to add value by taking genuine ownership of IT problems and deliver robust solutions, providing them with seasoned and hands-on CIO expertise in designing and executing the most relevant IT strategy.

Every company's mission is to create and protect shareholders value, but some clearly do a better job of it than others. While almost all companies have a vision of what they would like to accomplish, the biggest challenge lies in the execution.

As a senior executive, you want your IT organization to deliver business solutions that create, capture, and commercialize value throughout the entire enterprise. How relevant is IT for your overall corporate strategy? How would you rate the value delivered by your IT organization? How would you rate your IT spending as percentage of sales versus the industry in which you compete?

Our immediate results commitment to our clients brings a step change improvement in efficiency and, more importantly, incremental value (i.e., revenue growth, operating margin, asset efficiency, and IT risk management) at exceptional rates.

Our clients turn to CIO Eureka! whenever they have critical needs to find "business relevance" in IT. They use us in a variety of capacities:

1. To benefit from our "hands on" CIO practice, we go beyond the traditional consulting job and provide an experienced, interim "CIO on loan" to lead with an "insiders" market knowledge and—more importantly—we deliver results and solutions.
2. To expand products and services, and to optimize operations.
3. To drive competitive advantage through IT innovation.

We deliver business value!

About the Author

José Ignacio Sordo Galarza
CIO Eureka! Founder & Managing Director

JOSÉ IGNACIO is an international citizen who has lived on three continents. He is an entrepreneurial, highly accomplished, award-winning global IT executive and CIO.

He started his career with The Procter & Gamble Company in Mexico and was later transferred to the Latin American headquarters in Caracas, Venezuela, where he became the regional CIO responsible for fourteen markets and 2,200 direct reports and seven-figure budgets. He has proven ability to direct successful global business-driven IT solutions and mergers and acquisitions.

He was transferred to Ohio in the summer of 2006. He led a global initiative to enhance P&G's distinctive customer-facing go-to-market capabilities, while increasing sales productivity among 10,000 sales associates in over 150 countries. With a genuine interest in understanding the needs of P&G's key global partners, he led a systems strategy to consolidation of separate (local) systems into a manageable portfolio of fewer, (global) solutions, which translated into more effective selling and incremental revenue. He also launched P&G's Global Shopper Based Services to enhance solutions in terms of broader access to shopper insights and allowing efficient analytics for almost all customer teams around the world.

Throughout his twenty-five-year career at Procter & Gamble, José Ignacio held leadership positions in multiple functions (commercial, supply chain, consumer market research, IT, and global shared services), and worked with the top five global retailers (Walmart, Carrefour, Tesco, Target, Metro), as well as with distributors and small independent stores.

He is frequently recognized within the industry for blending business acumen and IT strategy. He was named to HITEC 100 America's Most Influential Hispanics in Information Technology in 2008, 2009, 2010, and 2011.

His board experience includes:

1. Industry co-chairman of CECRAL (LatAm ECR Association)

2. Advisory Board Member for Transora in South America

3. Mentorship chair at HITEC's Board of Directors

4. Member of i.c.Stars* (Chicago) Program Committee

5. Co-chairman IERG (International Executives Resources Group) Chicago chapter

José Ignacio is a graduate of the Instituto Tecnológico y de Estudios Superiores de Monterrey (ITESM), Mexico, with a B.S. in computer science. He resides in Chicago, IL, with his wife and three children.

José Ignacio Sordo Galarza LinkedIn Profile:
www.linkedin.com/in/sordoji

PRAISE FOR *THE UNCOMFORTABLE CEO*™

I have concluded that it is too late to have an IT strategy. Now, companies must have a strategy that includes IT. This is your chance to get an inside view of how one very sensitive and global IT leader thinks and writes. Be prepared for something different from a typical business book. This book makes the case for listening to your IT folks and the book gives you a preview of what they will say.
~Bob Johansen
Distinguished Fellow, Institute for the Future
Author of *Leaders Make the Future*

The Uncomfortable CEO™ *is the ideal playbook for CEOs and other business leaders who want to harness the power of IT to its maximum. Through this book, José Ignacio explains and reinforces the frequently undermined principle that helping IT deliver real business value and become fully engaged and leveraged is a responsibility that should be shared between the CEO and Executive Management, not just the CIO.*
~Sanjog Aul
Founder and Show Host, CIO Talk Radio

I was very impressed. The book was very easy to read and understand. It makes a lot of common business sense…we struggle with the challenge (new data standards, old business processes, and new information technology, etc.), but realize that we would not be able to run our business without all of our systems working together. Good business reading!
~Miguel Angel Lopera
President & CEO, GS1 Global Office, The Global Language of Business

Becoming too comfortable is a C-suite recipe for business disruption. José Ignacio provides sound objectivity and perspective for executive leadership in this digitally connected business era. The insightful content on information sharing, business partnership, enabling decision making, managing complexity, and leadership resiliency make The Uncomfortable CEO™ *a valuable and very beneficial read.*
~Haden A. Land
Vice President, Engineering & Chief Technology Officer, Lockheed Martin Corporation

As the CEO, you may have an unprecedented number of options to consider, unique business challenges to face, and tough choices to make to stay ahead of competition. This is your everyday life! In this book, you will learn how information technology executives will help you deliver better business results by unleashing profitable new capabilities, simplifying business processes, and integrating work—internally and externally—with your business partners!
~Mariano Martin Mampaso
Vice Chairman of the Board, DIA
Former Global President of Sales, The Procter & Gamble Company

In business, and usually in life, if you are feeling comfortable for too long, something is wrong... one thing is being happy and another is being satisfied. Successful IT leaders should be leading their companies to a better place, not only keeping up with constant change. This is why I enjoyed reading my very good friend's book...a wake-up call for all leaders who are feeling comfortable...and satisfied.
~Leopoldo Coronado
Chief Operating Officer, Intcomex

The Uncomfortable CEO™ describes in practical terms the challenges and paradigms any CEO is facing in today's constantly changing markets. I wish I had had this book years ago when I became CEO. The reading would have saved me many hours of work attempting to decipher IT in plain business terms, specifically as it relates to its very relevant role in a strategic plan. Highly recommended reading for those who are already uncomfortable CEOs!
~J. L. Brake
Executive Vice President Latin America, Strategic Planning & Business Synergies
Laureate International Universities

There are many Basics in life: personal, relationships, organizations. These Basics are often very simple in principle—even though they may be very complex in practice/implementation. Without a knowledge and understanding of the relevant Basics, we cannot be effective in overall goal accomplishment. The Uncomfortable CEO™ describes a rich and fertile field for mining out and applying the Basics in a simple form. Value-creation is one of those basics and is correctly identified as such in this interesting read.
~Dr. Durward Hofler
Emeritus Professor of Management, Northeastern Illinois University

The Uncomfortable CEO™ is a straight-forward primary on the leadership concepts that resolve this dilemma. From understanding how to create meaningful value to creating a culture of innovation, this is a thought-provoking how-to for business executives of all functions.
~Robert D. Scott
Director, Center for Engineering Diversity & Outreach
Information Systems Executive Forum, University of Michigan

The Uncomfortable CEO™ opened my eyes to a commonly missed opportunity in innovation. Having been involved in a countless number of innovation projects, I can testify that a large majority of identified opportunities contain a technology component. The worst part is that most innovation teams, as diverse as they are, don't include IT representation. It is also true that it is important to have the CIO at the table during strategic innovation discussions; not only can this support the innovation infrastructure for the organization, but it can also bring a new level of relevance to the project portfolio that the IT organization is managing. Every innovation leader interested in being successful should read The Uncomfortable CEO™.
~Moisés Noreña
Global Director of Innovation, Whirlpool Corporation

Managing business complexity is challenging because, as executives, we are built to be control freaks. Your executive leadership team, including your CIO, should dive into it and then come back with the vision, direction, and decisions needed to overcome business uncertainty required to manage innovation. José Ignacio explains this in a unique and simple way in his fascinating book.
~Jorge Zavala
Chief Disruptive Officer, Technology Business Accelerator (TechBA), Silicon Valley

No one has jumped from a plane in a parachute or rafted down a river for the comfort of it. When a company decides to overcome doubts and fears related to leaving a comfortable business model, to embark upon a disruptive journey, the difference between conquering a new land and being a shipwrecked falls upon the team, the tools and plans for this adventure. José Ignacio has successfully summarized many of the key elements of the fundamental relationship that exists between a successful organization and the supporting business processes that today are intrinsically built on top of information technology. So please do not stay at the comfortable level of finding high-level, easy-to-grab ideas; rather, dig into the rich details and tools they propose to transform your organization.
~José Angel Arias
Global VicePresident of Business Innovation, Softtek

Winning in today's business environment requires not only sound strategies, the right leaders leading complex business decisions, and a major focus on operational discipline and execution, but also calls for leveraging information technology as a major enabler of innovation and value-creation. José Ignacio will show you the importance of challenging paradigms and keeping you uncomfortable in pursuit of better and simpler business solutions if you want to outpace your competition. Great reading and a wonderful learning opportunity!
~Cyro Gazola
**Senior Vice President & GM Brazil, Philips Consumer Lifestyle
Former Sales General Manager Latin America, The Procter & Gamble Company**

The digital world is the cornerstone of modern business, in order to compete effectively in a technology-driven environment organizations must be innovative, agile, connected, and customer-driven. In **The Uncomfortable CEO**™*, José Ignacio offers valuable insight on how to unleash IT as a key engine of innovation and value-creation, and how to charter these to build the pipeline that integrates the Corporation with the new market dynamic.*
~Alfonso R. Luna
**CEO, Kentriki Inc.
Latin America Marketing Director, Google
Andean Region Director, Microsoft**

A book for the C-level who wants to make history, and not simply hold on to a job. José Ignacio focuses on the importance of being bold, daring, and leading with confidence, as well as with conviction. It is a reminder of what the role and responsibility of a CEO should be amid the changing global business reality.
~Mona Pearl
**Founder & COO, BeyondAStrategy Inc.
Author, *Grow Globally***

The Uncomfortable CEO™ provides an excellent perspective of the value that information technology should provide to your business. From a leadership contribution standpoint, I really enjoyed the way the CIO job is depicted as being a "Resilient Leader," setting winning direction, listening well, and more importantly, not about doing one thing very well, but more about flexibility and diversity of thought. This is all about agility and out-playing your marketplace competitors!
~Gerardo Diaz
Owner and Senior Consultant, HPI México

This is a business book to be read, to learn, and more importantly, to put into practice. José Ignacio has built awareness and understanding among C-level executives and the IT professionals at par with the market demands of the 21st century.
~Ana Rodríguez
President and Founder, Semillas Consultores & Vía Bonum DH3

Cutting-edge IT is rarely safe and is not meant to be comfortable. In my opinion, the most informed executive in an organization is the CIO, who is the least understood and most under-utilized resource in the C-suite. In The Uncomfortable CEO™, the author directly addresses and guides non-IT executives as to how to use IT resources strategically for business intelligence and innovation, and how to accelerate profitable growth. The Uncomfortable CEO™ is critical reading for executives in the knowledge age.
~Praveen Gupta
Author of *The Innovation Solution*
Director, Center for Innovation Science, Illinois Institute of Technology, Chicago

In today's global business environment, anyone in a leadership role will benefit from reading The Uncomfortable CEO™. José Ignacio has provided valuable insight and motivation for leaders to effectively utilize information technology and improve their companies' performance. I will recommend this book to my consulting clients.
~James L. Waite
President, Ops Asia

It is much better for you to make yourself uncomfortable, rather than having your competition do it. Every organization needs to work on making its products/services obsolete by new business propositions they develop, instead of discovering that the competition has done it for them. This book approaches this paradigm in a very simple and straightforward way, making it very easy to understand and apply to everyday business decisions.
~Julio Ibarra
Procurement Global Supply Chain Operations, Starbucks

I love the book's message about being uncomfortable! I consistently tell all the i.c.stars grads, "Change is uncomfortable." That's how we know it is working and if we want to be change agents in business and in our communities, we must embrace the change in our lives to build empathy for those who will be introduced to the change we are making.
~Sandee Kastrul
President, i.c.stars

Can technology minimize uncertainty, as Everett Rogers once claimed? José Ignacio believes that it can when all things are properly aligned. His is an interesting and thought-provoking book for seasoned professionals to take stock and for aspiring executives to take notice.
~Dr. Pablo G. Molina
CIO, Georgetown University

This book is a must read for uncomfortable CEOs, it addresses the challenges that most executives have in understanding how IT can deliver incremental value to the business. José Ignacio provides a great perspective on how to make your organization sufficiently uncomfortable and drive innovation though IT by reducing business complexity. The fantastic insights and the way this book is written lead me to believe that it will become an icon in the business leadership community.
~José Luis Garza
Managing Director–Mexico, Microsoft

The gap between IT and Business is cyclical. Forty years ago companies that embraced IT as a strategic differentiator crushed rivals. This differentiation required custom software running on proprietary systems. Then came the rise of the off the shelf software including SAP, Oracle, Salesforce. com, etc. All businesses had access to the same software and hardware and IT became viewed as 'plumbing.' The author points out today there can be huge ROI from IT investments that drive business goals. The challenge is for the uncomfortable CEOs to team up with key IT thought leaders using a value-creation mindset. José Ignacio offers proven ways to do this.
~John Burrell
Sales–Chicago, Datalink

Beware of that warm-bath feeling—if you are feeling too comfortable, you are not going to get the best results, and you are vulnerable.
~Edward Jardine
Former Andean Vice President, The Procter & Gamble Company

As an international advisor to Fortune 500 corporations with 35 years of experience, I believe this book provides good business insights. Trying to describe "IT value" in the business is like pointing to a snowflake and asking someone to grasp the concept of downhill skiing. If José Ignacio were an athlete, this book would be his Winter Olympic Games' gold medal.
~Ramón Galarza Chardi
President and CEO, A.G. Consultores

The Uncomfortable CEO™ is a handbook, both enjoyable to read and actionable, for CEOs and other senior executives. This handbook lays out the argument, while providing guidance, for leveraging IT more significantly to drive business success as we move further into the 21st century. José Ignacio challenges IT to create value and be measured like everyone else.
~Rick Julien
Retired Partner, Crowe Horwath LLP

Today's business environment is an uncertain, fast changing world. Relying on proven business models is not sufficient anymore. The new world requires agility and constant transformation, based on new IT enabled business models and converting information into business insights. The CIO need to step up to the new reality, working with the CEO and his team, in making IT a strategic weapon for the company. This requires a CIO who is a business leader, deserving a "seat at the board table." The CIO can only deliver full value if the CEO is ready to unlock the strategic value IT can bring to the table. I have been working with Jose Ignacio for many years, and seen his suggestions in full action. So I am not surprised reading a very practical guide which I can highly recommend to CEOs AND CIOs. Failure to act on Jose Ignacio's suggestions might not yet spell disaster but certainly a missed opportunity to win big in today's highly competitive market.
~Stefan Walter Neff
Former Asia CIO and Shared Services, The Procter & Gamble Company

The Uncomfortable CEO™ epitomizes applied knowledge in the three dimensions of mastery: business, organization, and professional/IT to drive business results. It is also a journey into thinking as a strategist. Jose Ignacio takes a broad business view, draws information from diverse and varied sources, and importantly anticipates the future. He establishes meaningful connections that drive the business direction with the undeniable help of Information Technology. This book should be your beacon in the quest finding the real value of IT for your corporation.
~Rodrigo Roque
Legal Affairs Director, National Council of Science and Technology—Mexico (CONACYT)
Former Head, National Institute of Industrial Property—Mexico (IMPI)

One of the most important factors in leveraging technology is communicating it terms executive teams can relate to. José Ignacio speaks to this issue in his book.
~Rob West
Chief Security Officer, Intelligent ID
Former Chief Information Security Officer, Fifth Third Bank

In his book, The Uncomfortable CEO™, José Ignacio provides business CEOs with an effective road map— to be of true service, you must help IT professionals demonstrate the business value of their initiatives. Only by viewing their contributions as more than "commodity work," but as adding more force to the flow of ideas and information can suppliers and vendors help the streams become mighty rivers in industry or government. Hopefully, after reading this book, many business CEOs will also become "uncomfortable" and seek the answers and truths they need to make a significant difference in business and life, with its dead-on take of the reality facing CEOs and their love/hate relationships with the technology department. This is a "must read" book and I've urged our consortium's participating firms to get a copy ASAP.
~Harith Razaa
CEO and Founder, Minority Information Technology Consortium

When everybody feels comfortable, and you are the uncomfortable leader, you have a universe of opportunities. In other words, being uncomfortable is actually the source of ample opportunities. Corollary, being comfortable is indeed the source of many threats in the society.
~Dr. Andy Chen
Associate Professor of Management Information Systems, Northeastern Illinois University